Analysts, Lies, and Statistics

Cutting Through the Hype in Corporate Earnings Announcements

Analysts, Lies, and Statistics

Cutting Through the Hype in Corporate Earnings Announcements

Brian R. Bruce and Mark T. Bradshaw

Euromoney Institutional Investor

Published by
Institutional Investor Books
225 Park Avenue South
New York, NY 10003

Tel: US +1 800 437 9997 or 1 212 224 3570
Fax: 1 212 224 3671
Email: ushotline@iinvestor.net
Website: www.iibooks.com

ISBN 1 85564 974 8

Printed in England by Hobbs the Printers

Contents

About the authors

Brian R. Bruce is Director and Head of Equity Investments at PanAgora Asset Management. Brian is responsible for the research and management of the global active equity strategies at PanAgora. He is also a member of the firm's Management and Investment Committees. In addition, Brian is Visiting Professor of Investments at Baylor University. Prior to joining PanAgora, Brian simultaneously served as a Professor at Southern Methodist University's Cox Business School, and as President and Chief Investment Officer of Intercoast Capital, a subsidiary of a *Fortune* 500 energy company. Brian previously worked at State Street Global Advisors, the Northern Trust Company, and Stein Roe & Farnham.

Brian received a MBA from the University of Chicago, a MS in Computer Science from DePaul University, and a BS in Business Administration from Illinois State University. Brian is a member of the Illinois State University College of Business Hall of Fame, and is a winner of the University of Chicago Graduate School of Business CEO Award. He has published numerous scholarly articles and books, and is the Editor-in-Chief of Institutional Investor's *Journal of Investing*. Brian frequently appears in the media, including being interviewed by NBC, ABC, CNBC, the *Wall Street Journal*, the *Washington Post*, the *New York Times*, the *Financial Times*, *Business Week*, Associated Press, Reuters, and Bloomberg.

Mark T. Bradshaw is Assistant Professor at Harvard Business School, Harvard University. Mark recently joined the faculty as an Assistant Professor of Business Administration in the Accounting and Control Area. He teaches the first-year MBA course, Financial Reporting and Control. His research investigates how capital market intermediaries process financial statement data into forecasts of future earnings, derive current valuations, and generate investment recommendations.

Professor Bradshaw received his PhD from the University of Michigan Business School (Ann Arbor, Michigan) in 2000, and BBA and MAcc degrees from the University of Georgia (Athens, Georgia) in 1989 and 1995. He is a Certified Public Accountant, and previously worked for Arthur Andersen & Co. in the attestation services division of their Atlanta office from 1988 to 1994. While there, he specialized in publicly traded companies including Delta Air Lines, Continental Airlines, and The Southern Company, and private enterprises, including the Augusta National Golf Club, The Masters Golf Tournament, and the Institute of Nuclear Power Operators.

Preface

The creation and use of analyst data was a 'new truth' when it first appeared. The collection of this information has been one of the most important achievements of modern portfolio management. Up until now, the only book on the subject, *The Handbook of Corporate Earnings Analysis*, was a collection of articles edited by this book's co-author along with Chuck Epstein back in 1994. That book spawned the Corporate Earnings Analysis Seminar (CEAS) in 1996. CEAS brought practitioners, academics, and vendors together to share information and build a community. Now, almost 10 years later, the creator of CEAS, Brian Bruce, and one of CEAS's top contributors, Mark Bradshaw, have combined to write the first book on the history of, topics in, and uses of earnings estimates.

During the past 10 years, dramatic changes have occurred in the field. These changes are significant, and must be readily understood by anyone using earnings in their investment process. With so many people talking about earnings and their impact on stock prices, we felt the time was right to produce a book on the subject that would explain the changes in the field, and discuss how to take advantage of those changes when investing in the stock market.

It is hoped it is a useful book, and that you gain some insight into how earnings and earnings estimates are created and utilized. Further, it is hoped that you will be invigorated by the discussions and ideas included in this book.

We would like to thank all who helped with this project, including Allison Adams, Elizabeth Gray, Stan Levine, Haim Mozes, Ramu Tiagaragen, Amitabh Dugar, Nick Bird, John Geuard, Joe Gatto, and Deborah Trask. We also thank our colleagues at Harvard Business School and Panagora Asset Management for their support of this project. Our apologies to anyone we have forgotten.

Chapter 1

Introduction

It is the customary fate of new truths to begin as heresies and to end as superstitions.

Thomas Henry Huxley

The time is right for a book that addresses the use of earnings and earnings estimate data in picking stocks. The number of people using estimate data has grown over the past 15 years from a small group of fanatics to mainstream America. Ten years ago, did anyone know what earnings surprise was? Turn on CNBC during earnings season and you will hear the term used several times per hour. The speed at which this topic has moved from the fringe to the mainstream is nothing short of amazing. With all of the newfound emphasis on earnings estimates, the lack of a book covering this topic is an obvious gap in the literature of finance. This book will cover all of the topics necessary to understand the use of earnings estimate data. It starts with an overview section, which contains needed background material. The second section covers popular issues regarding the earnings and estimates. The final section shows how to utilize this information in picking stocks for your portfolio.

The book begins with an introductory section that discusses the history of earnings estimates and the roles they play. Chapter 2, 'The history of earnings estimates', discusses expectations of earnings. In this chapter, there is a brief stroll down memory lane, highlighting how earnings estimates have been collected and disseminated over the years. Understanding the basic process involved sets the stage for being able to understand how this data has been used and misused over the years, and provides insights into the best ways to utilize this valuable information.

In Chapter 3 there is an examination of the role that analysts play. Based on the recent accounting scandals, a reasonable investor might ask 'What role do analysts serve? Why can't we get rid of them? At the very least, let's replace them with independent research firms and not rely on analysts tied to brokerage firms.' This chapter shows the critical function that analysts play in the flow of information from companies to investors, and subsequent chapters show how to properly utilize information provided by analysts despite their limited accuracy. This chapter examines the role of those analysts, their motivations, and the amount of useful information they provide.

Chapter 4, 'Analysts' conflicts of interests', discusses sell-side analysts as a source of a number of primary pieces of information relevant to those wishing to effectively invest in common stocks. The analysts provide projections of earnings growth, purchase recommendations, target prices, and commentary on the possible risks and rewards of owning a particular stock. These analysts provide a critical link in the information flow between company and investor. It is examined how much faith you should place in the research reports and recommendations of analysts, given that they are essentially paid by the firms they are evaluating.

The book then focuses on all of the various topics which are part of the field. Chapter 5 focuses on various estimates of earnings growth. First, analysts forecast the level of earnings growth over longer term horizons. Second, they provide target prices, which are forecasts of actual price levels. Finally, they issue stock recommendations to buy or sell securities. Moving forward, they are starting to estimate sales and other income statement information that may be less likely to be involved in the generally accepted accounting principles (GAAP) versus Pro Forma earnings discussion (which is covered in the following chapter). In this chapter, these other items are considered, and we discuss how useful these metrics are to investor stock-selection models.

In Chapter 6, the focus changes from looking at the various estimates being made, and moves into that of which those estimates are comprised. For years, investors have focused their attention on earnings calculated in accordance with GAAP established by the regulatory organizations and their predecessors (GAAP). However, recently companies have been reporting an ever widening array of alternatively calculated earnings figures, and Wall Street has embraced these definitions of earnings, although these are not explicitly defined or sanctioned by any of the regulatory overseers. These definitions are known by such names as 'pro forma,' 'normalized,' 'cash earnings,' and a host of other such names. In this chapter, there is an examination of this trend, and we provide two sides of the argument for and against the use of pro forma accounting numbers. The chapter looks at whether investors should pay attention to these numbers, or should they view them as an attempt by managers to hoodwink them into believing earnings are rosier than they are?

After looking at estimates and what makes them up, Chapter 7, 'Earnings management', addresses the question 'Do managers manipulate earnings?' Almost anyone familiar with the financial reporting process would not hesitate to answer the question posed above. Most people would respond, 'Yes, of course managers manage earnings'. However, what does it mean, to 'manage' earnings? Most observers would agree that any deliberate intervention in the accounting process aimed at affecting reported financial numbers would fall under the definition of earnings management. However, there seems to be no accepted definition of earnings management. Nevertheless, there seems to be a general consensus among academics, regulators, and the investment community that earnings manipulation is characterized by managerial intent to paint a picture of firm performance that is not accurate. Additionally, most believe that earnings management is widespread. However, is there hard evidence to support this claim? Why would managers care so much about managing earnings? How can it be measured whether earnings have been managed? What has been documented regarding the pervasiveness of earnings management? In this chapter, there is a very brief description of how researchers have viewed earnings management, and we summarize a small but representative sampling of the evidence.

Chapter 7 also examines the impact of pre-announcements. In the ancient times before earnings surprise (any time before 1995) was discussed on CNBC and available on web sites, there was little violent one day reaction of stock prices to earnings news. In the modern days since those times, 25% one day price movements in reaction to earnings announcements occur regularly. As corporate management does not enjoy large negative price movements, the practice of pre-announcements has become prevalent. Management hopes that by sharing potential negative news the price reaction to announcements would be more restrained. Pre-announcements have quickly become part of the landscape. First Call has started collecting data on pre-announcements and research is being done on the data.

Chapter 8 looks at the topic which is the focus of the most cutting edge research today, 'Accruals and earnings quality'. In the chapters preceding this one, there is a consideration of the uses of estimates of earnings. This chapter looks in-depth at the earnings being estimated. It starts by looking at earnings quality, and then earnings management and pro forma earnings. This analysis should give investors a better idea of which earnings estimates have a greater likelihood of occurring, and which do not. Let's start with quality. Analysts forecast earnings, but it is cash flows that ultimately matter. There is a lot of misunderstanding about the link between earnings and cash flows. Simply stated, the difference between earnings and cash flows reflects accounting accruals. In this chapter, there is a brief consideration of this link. Then, there is a discussion of how investors can take advantage of an understanding of this link to identify stocks that will likely report earnings reversals.

Up to this point, this book has focused on the estimates made by analysts that are sent to the data collectors. What about estimates of future earnings that are generated but are not collected by the data services? Does finding them and using them provide any informational advantage? Chapter 9 examines this question by analyzing 'Whisper estimates'. Whisper estimates became popular in the 1990s. They are the natural outgrowth of the behavioral adjustments that continually occur in the earnings estimate cycle. When estimates were first collected by I/B/E/S, there was no need to whisper. People barely paid attention to the published estimates. By the mid 1980s, use of estimates in managing institutional money began to proliferate. So when the technology bubble hit in the late 1990s, estimate data was so popular that it appeared on websites aimed at individual investors. When published estimates become common knowledge, the next step in the behavioral cycle is to try to get better or faster information than the estimate. This led to the growth of whisper estimates, which are examined in depth.

In Chapter 10, there is an examination of the question 'Are there superior analysts?' Do analysts at large firms or who are 'Institutional Investor All-Americans' predict earnings any better than the average? In this chapter, the evidence is considered on the existence of superior analysts. As it turns out, depending on how you measure 'superior,' there do seem to be certain analysts who are better than others. There is also a consideration of research that concludes that not only does the market believe that there are superior analysts, but that the market gives more weight to forecasts, recommendations, and target prices of superior analysts, resulting in stronger market reactions to their announcements.

The book then looks at the tools used by portfolio managers, and the integration of those tools into an equity process. So far, there has been an examination of the history of earnings estimates, the role of analysts, and the use of estimate data in looking at earnings surprises. Chapter 11 focuses on a tool utilized by professional money managers: earnings revisions. The ability to use a large number of estimates by professional money managers in a formal way has led to the creation of the earnings revision model. This model was the first structured use of expectational data. In fact, the earnings revision model was the first successful use of behavioral finance concepts in portfolio management (although, at the time these models were created, behavioral finance did not exist as a field of study).

In Chapter 12 there is an examination of what 'earnings surprise' is. It is an earnings announcement that differs from what analysts were expecting. Earnings surprise often causes a substantial movement in the stock's price. In the 1960s, the concept of earnings surprise was limited to a few academics doing research on an effect that was not known to many sophisticated investors. Now there is an examination of why it seems to be covered everywhere.

Up to this point, the book has discussed many facets of earnings and estimates of earnings. Chapter 13 is the appropriate close to this book, showing how to integrate earnings into a portfolio management strategy. One of the most difficult tasks a portfolio manager faces is making his or her product unique. This requires lots of creativity, as so many people utilize a small number of ideas. How do you make your process unique while not discussing the sources of your inspiration? In this case, the sources include the hundreds of academic papers that have been written on this subject. Other sources are the dozens of fabulous speakers who have appeared over the years at the Corporate Earnings Analysis Seminar (www.Investment research.org). Additional sources are all of the portfolio managers who have tried to use this data over the years.

Finally, in Chapter 14, some final thoughts on the subject are provided. This is a rich and ever-changing field. There can be no real conclusion, just a current summary of where we are in understanding the effects of earnings on stock prices. Hopefully, this volume will help with your understanding of how to use earnings in evaluating companies for investment.

Chapter 2

The history of earnings estimates

It is no great wonder if in long process of time, while fortune takes her course hither and thither, numerous coincidences should spontaneously occur.

Plutarch

Expectations of earnings have been around for as long as firms have been generating them. For example, Graham and Dodd's classic security analysis, which has been historically thought of as the 'bible' of financial analysts, devotes substantial attention to the analysis of earnings for purposes of assessing future earnings. However, the massive infrastructure for the forecasting of earnings that is seen today is like nothing seen in the past. In fact, the notion of a 'consensus' earnings estimate is relatively new. It took an increased focus on stocks by individuals during the tech bubble of the late 1990s to bring the concept of consensus to popularity. The subsequent fallout from the earnings accounting scandals focused even more attention on earnings and earnings forecasts. These watershed events, combined with the increasing availability of low cost technology and the widespread dissemination of earnings forecasts, has caused earnings forecasts to be one of the premier determinants of stock prices. In this chapter, there is a brief stroll down memory lane, and we highlight how earnings estimates have been collected and disseminated over the years. Understanding the basic process involved sets the stage for being able to understand how this data has been used and misused over the years, and provides insights into the best ways to utilize this valuable information.

Changes in the timeliness of information

Let's begin by focusing on the mechanics of data and its collection. Investors have used data since the days of Graham and Dodd. However, it is a relatively recent phenomenon, propelled by increasing computer power and the internet, for vast amounts of data to be available to such a large number of investors. One of the most important changes that has occurred during the past 25 years is that the timeliness of data on market and firm specific earnings information has improved to the point that, effectively, many of the estimates reach clients in real-time. It is important to realize that, for most of the time that earnings forecasts have been collected, they have been entered into the databases anywhere from a week to several months after they were made.

During the 1970s through the mid 1980s, it usually took several weeks or longer from the time that an analyst made an estimate to the time that the estimates services clients received the estimates. In those years, estimates were manually entered into the estimates services databases from printed monthly statistical summaries. This was usually done in a day or two. Sometimes, during a crunch, or if documents were particularly long (like Merrill Lynch's Monthly Research Review), it may have taken several days.

The steps an estimate goes through in its passage from analyst to estimates services client are:

- analyst makes estimate;
- broker publishes estimate;
- broker sends estimate to estimates service;
- estimates service calculates summary statistics; and
- estimates service publishes estimate.

To make the timeliness issue graphically clear, hypothetical examples of this process in the late 1980s will be shown. By comparison, a recent case of real-time analyst response to an earnings announcement on First Call from 1996 will be shown.

Estimate revision process: 1980s

Let us follow the passage of two hypothetical estimates from origination by the analyst to publication by the estimates service, as it would have occurred in the late 1980s. In the best case, the estimate would have been published by the estimates service eight days after the analyst made the estimate. In the worst case, this would have taken 43 days.

In the best case, Day 0 is just before the deadline for the estimate to be included in the broker's Monthly Statistical Summary (MSS), and the estimates service receives the MSS before its weekly deadline (see Exhibit 2.1).

In the worst case, Day 0 is the day after the deadline for the estimate to be included in the broker's MSS, and the estimates service receives the MSS one day after the deadline for the estimates service's weekly publication (see Exhibit 2.2).

In Exhibit 2.2, two estimates made one day apart would have had system entry dates in the estimates database 35 days apart. If the publication dates of the MSS were used to date the estimates, then the estimates would have been dated roughly 30 days apart.

Exhibit 2.1

Estimate revision process: best case

Day	
0	Analyst makes estimate.
1	After editing, MSS goes to press at broker.
2	Broker mails MSS.
4	Estimates service receives MSS (on Thursday before weekly production). Estimates service enters estimate in database.
5	Estimate is included in summary statistics calculated Thursday night.
6	Estimate is included in printed report over the weekend.
8	Client receives printed reports Monday morning. Summary data is available on time-sharing service.

Source: Authors' own.

6

Exhibit 2.2

Estimate revision process: worst case

Day	
0	Analyst makes estimate.
30	After editing, MSS goes to press at broker.
31	Broker mails MSS.
33	Estimates service receives MSS (on a Friday after weekly production run).
36	Estimates service enters estimate in database.
40	Estimate is included in summary statistics calculated Thursday night.
41	Estimate is included in printed report over the weekend.
43	Client receives printed reports Monday morning. Summary data is available on time-sharing service.

Source: Authors' own.

The above example would have applied under the best of circumstances in those days. The best of circumstances would have required the following.

- The broker suffered no delays in getting the MSS to press.
- The broker suffered no delays in printing the MSS.
- There were no delays in delivering the MSS to the estimates service, and the broker remembered to send the MSS to the estimates service (brokers often forgot).
- The estimates service suffered no delays in entering the estimate into database. (Under certain circumstances, a one day delay in entering the data could result in a four day delay in the estimate entering the database, and a seven day delay in the estimate's inclusion in the summary statistics).
- The estimates service suffered no production delays (an infrequent occurrence).
- The estimates service suffered no delays in printing publications, or in getting files to the time-sharing service.

Often, the above conditions were not met. This resulted in delays of over 36 days for an estimate's inclusion in the estimates service's database.

Estimate revision process: 1996 and beyond

Now let's see how things work today. The following real-time example illustrates the speed with which estimates reach First Call after an event. In the following example:

At 4:13 PM (eastern time) on 15 April 1996, Sanmina Corp. reported second quarter earnings of 38 cents. This was two cents above the First Call consensus. The company also announced a stock split. This prompted analysts to immediately raise their estimates. Here is what happened:

7

1. Sanmina Corp. report received by NewsEDGE at 4:31 PM.[1]

Sanmina Reports Record Second Quarter Results; Randy Furr Promoted To President And Chief Operating Officer

   SAN JOSE, Calif.—(BUSINESS WIRE)—April 15, 1996—Sanmina Corporation, a leading contract manufacturer, today reported operating results for the second quarter and six months ended March 30, 1996.

   Second quarter 1996 highlights include:
Record revenues; increase 61% versus Q2 1995
Fully diluted EPS 36 cents versus 23 cents Q2 1995
Two-for-one stock split effective March 11, 1996
New North Carolina facility begins shipping product

16:13 ET APR 15, 1996

BW0270 APR 15,1996 13:13 PACIFIC 16:13 EASTERN
:TICKER: SANM
:SUBJECT: SEMI COFF CA EARN
Copyright (c) 1996 Business Wire

Received by NewsEDGE/LAN: 4/15/96 4:31 PM

---

2. Broker notes start coming into First Call at 7:19 AM the next morning (April 16). The last note comes in at 3:00 PM. Five of the nine analysts send notes through First Call.[1]

03:00pm EDT 16-Apr-96 Cowen & Co. (COWEN & COMPANY) INTC IFMX TRW NELL HDTC NN
MORNING MEETING NOTE, APRIL 16, 1996

01:48pm EDT 16-Apr-96 J.C. Bradford & Co. (BILL CAGE (615) 748-9319) SANM
SANM: 2Q EPS BETTER THAN EXPECTED

11:03am EDT 16-Apr-96 Montgomery Securities (P. Fox (415) 627-2012) SANM
SANM: 2Q BEATS EXPECTATIONS; RAISING ESTIMATES AND PRICE TARGET

10:45am EDT 16-Apr-96 Hambrecht & Quist (Todd D. Bakar, 415-576-3316) SANM CSCO
Sanmina Corp.: Strong FQ2 Results Above Expectations; Raising Projections

09:34am EDT 16-Apr-96 Cowen & Co. (ROB STONE/DANIEL BLAKE) SANM
SANM/ UPSIDE QTR., DESPITE GOODWILL + STARTUP COSTS 4 2 PLANTS

09:00am EDT 16-Apr-96 First Call Earnings Surprise PRIZE SGO EUSA CMPC ARVX BLT
Significant Surprises – Consensus EPS vs. Reported EPS 04:45pm – 08:45am

07:19am EDT 16-Apr-96 Morgan Stanley (Fleck, Shelby (212) 761-6408) SANM
SANMINA CORP. RAISING ESTIMATES AND PRICE TARGET

---

3. Here, as an example, is the last note that comes into First Call at 3:00 PM on April 16, from Cowen & Co.[1]

03:00pm EDT 16-Apr-96 Cowen & Co. (COWEN & COMPANY) INTC IFMX TRW
NELL HDTC NN
MORNING MEETING NOTE, APRIL 16, 1996

COWEN & COMPANY
Drew Peck, Drew Brosseau, Cai von Rumohr, Dan Lemaitre, Steve Weber,
Jim Kedersha, Richard Chu, Joyce Lonergan, Elliott Rogers, Rob Stone, Brian
Skiba, Maria Kussmaul Lewis
617-946-3700
4/16/96

Sanmina – Strong Buy   Sanmina – Strong Buy   Sanmina – Strong Buy
1996E $1.44 +0.08 Delivered another upside Q; raising price target from $37
1997E $1.71 +0.08 to $39. Q2 sales grew 61%, gross margin was better than
                  expected despite added goodwill and start-up costs for
                  two plants. There is room for further expansion in the U.S.
                  and SANM plans to enter Europe this year, adding upside.

SANM $30 – R.Stone.   SANM $30 – R.Stone.   SANM $30 – R.Stone.
COWEN & COMPANY BOSTON (617) 946-3700 NEW YORK (212) 495-6000
SAN FRANCISCO(415) 434-7800 CHICAGO (312) 704-7400 ALBANY (518)
463-5244 CLEVELAND (216)21-8300 DAYTON (513) 226-4800 HOUSTON
(713) 652-7100 TOKYO 813-3503-0371 TORONTO (416) 362-2229

---

4. Eight of nine First Call estimates are revised the next day (April 16). One estimate is revised a day later (April 17).[1]

FIRST CALL Earnings Estimates Summary for SANM SANMINA CORP.
Fiscal Year Ending Sep   Last Updated: 17-Apr-96 10:58am

Year Ending	Q1 Dec	Q2 Mar	Q3 Jun	Q4 Sep	Fisc Yr Annual	Num Brok
1997	0.40	0.43	0.44	0.47	1.73	9
1996	0.32A	0.36A	0.37	0.39	1.44	9

Consensus Recommendation: 1.1 Consensus Future 5-yr Growth Rate: 25%

FIRST CALL Earnings Estimates   SANM
Fiscal Year Ending Sep 96   Last Updated: 17-Apr-96

Brokers	Q1 Dec-95	Q2 Mar-96	Q3 Jun-96	Q4 Sep-96	Fisc Yr Annual	Fisc Yr Last Rev/Orig
Stephens Inc.:	0.32A	0.36A	0.36	0.39	1.41	17-Apr-96
Previous:	0.28	0.33	0.34	0.37	1.39	
Cowen & Co.:	0.32A	0.36A	0.37	0.39	1.44	16-Apr-96
Previous:	0.30	0.33	0.34	0.36	1.36	

Montgomery:	0.32A	0.36A	0.37	0.39	1.45	16-Apr-96
Previous:	0.30	0.34	0.36	0.38	1.38	
Morgan Stanley:	0.32A	0.36A	0.37	0.39	1.44	16-Apr-96
Previous:	0.31	0.34	0.34	0.38	1.38	
J.C. Bradford:	0.32A	0.36A	0.37	0.39	1.44	16-Apr-96
Previous:	0.30	0.34	0.36	0.38	1.39	
Needham & Co.:	0.32A	0.36A	0.37	0.39	1.44	16-Apr-96
Previous:	0.30	0.34	0.36	0.38	1.40	
Genesis:	0.32A	0.36A	0.38	0.40	1.45	16-Apr-96
Previous:	0.31	0.34	0.35	0.38	1.39	
Adams Harkness:	0.32A	0.36A	0.37	0.39	1.44	16-Apr-96
Previous:	–	0.33	0.35	0.37	1.36	
Hambrecht:	0.32A	0.36A	0.37	0.39	1.44	16-Apr-96
Previous:	0.30	0.34	0.36	0.38	1.40	
RTEE Actual:	0.32A	0.36A	–	–	–	15-Apr-96
FIRST CALL Consensus Statistics [9 Brokers]						
Current Mean:	0.32A	0.36A	0.37	0.39	1.44	17-Apr-96
Previous Mean:	0.30	0.34	0.35	0.38	1.38	
Standard Dev:	0.01	0.01	0.00	0.00	0.01	
Report Date:	01/15A	04/15A	07/17w	10/28w		

How did this happen? The above examples illustrate the remarkable changes in procedures by the brokerage houses and estimates services. Through the use of improved computer and communications technology, and spurred on by competition, the estimates services are now much more timely than they were in the past.

Over the years the following technological innovations came into common use:

- fax;
- extraction of estimates from real-time notes, transmitted over telephone lines;
- electronic file transmission;
- improved procedures by the estimates services for entering and checking data; and
- electronic transmission of estimates, as they are made.

Receipt of estimates by the estimates services became more frequent:

- the monthly printed reports were supplemented with weekly reports;
- then with daily faxes;
- then with monthly, weekly and daily electronic transmissions;
- then with real time extraction of estimates from broker notes developed by First Call; and
- then with real time transmissions of estimate revisions developed by First Call.

The changes started taking place in the years indicated below:

- 1984: tape files;
- 1986: floppy disks;

- 1987: fax;
- 1988: electronic file transfers;
- 1988: real time (daily) input from broker notes initiated by First Call; and
- 1990: real time transmission of analyst estimates initiated by First Call.

Today, in the worst case, it might take over a month for an estimate revision to make it into one of these estimate databases. This is the exception, however, and is not acceptable. In the best cases, the estimates are in the databases on a real-time basis.

Summary

In this chapter, it has been shown how the data collection and publication process of the estimates services has changed over the years. The most dramatic changes have taken place during the past five years. The researchers who have used these databases have not recognized this factor. This suggests research to determine the effect that precise dating would have on previous conclusions arrived at with imprecise estimate dates. Due to this, the following observations are made.

- In this book there is a discussion of utilizing estimate revision and estimate surprise models in portfolio management. With better data, estimate revision and surprise studies (and subsequent models) most likely yield better results. By using the precisely dated files from First Call, we may be able to gain insight into changing investor behavior. Using data that is changing over time makes it difficult to unravel the changing quality of the estimates data over time from that of investor behaviors. We can see that market participants respond more quickly to estimate revisions now than they did in the past.
- Studies of the accuracy of analysts estimates will probably find analysts to be more accurate than previous studies have indicated.
- Analyst quality studies done with the First Call database might yield clearer indications that there are superior analysts, and make for better ways of identifying them.

First Call recently assembled an Earnings Estimates History database going back to 1989. The Williams and Mozes paper is the first serious academic study done with this database.[2] Williams and Mozes drew conclusions that differed from O'Brien's earlier work with the I/B/E/S historic files.[3] Perhaps if O'Brien had done her work with more precisely dated estimates, she would have found, as Williams and Mozes did, that the most recent estimate revision is often a laggard, and not the most accurate.

This serves as an example of how research with precisely timed estimates data may change the picture we have of analyst behavior, and the effect of securities analysts on stock prices. There now follows a consideration of the critical role that analysts play in the investment process.

---

[1] *Source:* First Call.

[2] Mozes, Haim A., and Patricia Williams (2000), 'Brokerage Firm Analysts: How Good Are the Forecasts?', *The Journal of Investing*, Fall, Vol. 9, No. 3, pp. 5–13.

[3] O'Brien, Patricia C. (1998), 'Analysts Forecasts as Earnings Expectations', *Journal of Accounting and Economics*, January, Vol. 10, No. 1, pp. 55–83.

Chapter 3

The role of analysts

Q: Why didn't Wall Street realize that Enron was a fraud?

A: Because Wall Street relies on stock analysts. These are people who do research on companies and then, no matter what they find, even if the company has burned to the ground, enthusiastically recommend that investors buy the stock.

Dave Barry

Quotes like the above from Dave Barry signify the dissatisfaction of most investors with analysts. After the technology bubble burst, the fallout hit many high profile analysts. The following period of accounting scandals has led to even less investor confidence in analysts. A reasonable investor might ask 'What role do analysts serve? Why can't we get rid of them? At the very least, let's replace them with independent research firms and not rely on analysts tied to brokerage firms.' In this chapter, the critical function that analysts play in the flow of information from companies to investors is considered, and subsequent chapters show how to properly utilize information provided by analysts despite their limited accuracy.

Investors generally rely on the opinions of experts (or other experts besides ourselves) to help us pick stocks. Whether an investor buys stocks through a 401(k) plan or a mutual fund, they utilize expert opinion of both portfolio managers and stock analysts. Recent scandals such as Enron have caused these analysts to be much maligned. This book examines the role of those analysts, their motivations, and the amount of useful information they provide.

Buy and sell recommendations

Recently, analyst recommendations have been subject to much scrutiny. The best place to start looking at those recommendations is the overall recommendation from analysts. Each analyst issues a strong buy, buy, hold, sell or strong sell recommendation for each stock that they follow. What did each of three leading compilers of earnings estimate data show with their data recently?

Thompson Financial/First Call aggregated these recommendations in July of 2001, and found that almost 50% of all recommendations were buy, while less than 1% were sell. A similar study done by Zacks Investment Research of over 8,000 recommendations of stocks in the S&P 500 showed that only 29 were sells, or less than 0.5%. This compared to 214 strong buy recommendations.

The third firm, I/B/E/S, had their data analyzed in a study by Li (2002) over time. It showed startling consistency across seven years and nearly a quarter million recommendations (see Exhibit 3.1).

This pattern cannot appear by chance. Consistently averaging 2% of all recommendations as sells is not because only 2% of all companies followed are worthy of that recommendation. What causes analysts to have such a significant bias in their recommendations?

Exhibit 3.1

Changes in ratings, 1994–2000 (%)

I/B/E/S Rating	Strong buy	2	3	4	Sell	Total recommendations
1994	25	33	37	2	3	29,521
1995	27	32	36	2	3	30,854
1996	30	33	32	2	2	29,734
1997	31	37	29	1	2	30,350
1998	29	39	30	1	1	35,445
1999	30	40	28	2	1	37,318
2000	31	40	27	1	1	32,663
Average	29	36	32	2	2	

Source: Li (2002).

The analyst cycle and the critical role of analysts

To understand analyst recommendations, you first must understand the analyst cycle (see Exhibit 3.2). This cycle is a description of all the forces that act on analysts in their making of a recommendation. The first part is the source of much information to an analyst: company management. Company management provides financial projections about future earnings, and provides access to the analyst to members of company management to discuss the firm's prospects. In this part of the relationship, the analyst is a non-paying client of the company.

There is a second part to the relationship between company and analyst. Many analysts work for firms that are investment banks. Investment banks market to companies to do the companies' investment banking business, such as issuing bonds or a new class of stock. The relationship now may be that the company is the client to the analyst and his firm. Since the analyst works for the firm, he must not get in the way of the investment banking marketing effort, and, in fact, may be asked to help in that effort.

The next relationship is that of the analyst to the investor. The analyst provides the investor with critical information about a security that may be difficult to obtain by the investor. In return, the analyst needs the investor to trade with the analyst's firm in order for

Exhibit 3.2

Analyst earnings cycle

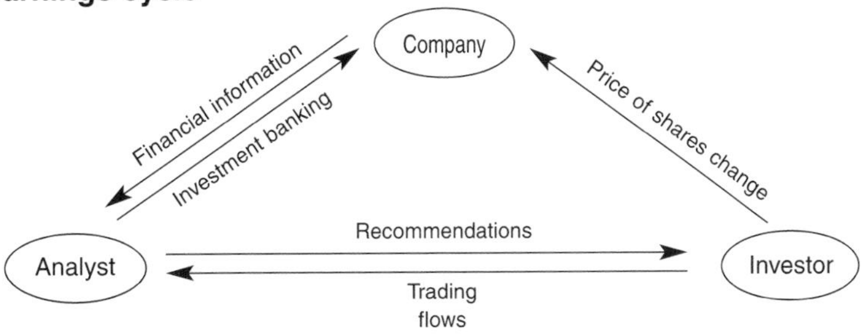

Source: Authors' own.

his/her firm to 'get paid'. Many times in a portfolio manager's career does he or she get a call from an analyst asking if the portfolio manager values the information that the analyst sends. If the portfolio manager answers yes, the analyst will generally ask for a certain level of trading commissions to flow to his/her firm. Many analysts are judged based on the amount of trading flow they bring into a firm.

Finally, there is the link back to the company. The investor will act on the information provided by the analyst (along with other information). This will affect the price, which is of great concern to company management. As stock options became more prevalent in the 1990s, the concern of senior management turned from earning a large cash bonus to getting lots of stock options, and maximizing their value. This causes senior management of a company to be very concerned about what investors think about the company.

The analyst conflict of interest

Why don't analysts issue sell recommendations? If they did, they may alienate a client of their firm and risk future investment banking business. Or they may simply be cut off from information flow about a firm. The recent case of AOL Time Warner is an excellent example of this. According to the published reports (Angwin and Peers, 2001), after downgrading AOL from a buy to a neutral rating Merrill Lynch analysts Henry Blodget and Jessica Reif Cohen were not able to communicate with the firm as they had in the past. Multiple phone calls were made by Henry Blodget, Jessica Reif Cohen, and their research assistants, and none were returned. In addition, meetings scheduled between the firm and the analysts were cancelled by AOL. The analysts firmly believe that they were put in the 'penalty box' by AOL for making a downgrade recommendation. This belief was based on a phone conversation with the Chief Financial Officer of AOL Time Warner, where he spoke harshly to the analysts, and said that he would not answer questions from them. The CFO also acknowledged that he complained to Merrill Lynch's investment bankers about the downgrade.

Another example is when investment banking firms try to utilize analysts as marketers. Lauricella (2001) describes the situation at Bear Sterns, where a bank stock analyst received a call from the head of the firm's bond trading desk. The trader wanted the analyst to start covering a small banking stock because it was a potential customer. Analysts claim that they are under heavy pressure to issue favorable ratings of firms that are investment banking or trading customers of the analyst's firm. This pressure can come in the form of phone calls or even direct compensation. Bear Sterns' analyst bonuses were based on the analysts ability to market their stock picks to institutional investors. Firms may even subject analyst's to scrutiny by instructing them 'to seek approval from corporate clients before publishing recommendations on those stocks'. This quote came from the head of equity research for Europe at JP Morgan.

Analysts readily admit that companies communicate with them much more freely when an analyst has issued a good recommendation on their stock. This type of reward and punishment behavior by companies has a strong effect on analysts. So why do they care so much? The answer is analyst compensation.

Becoming an analyst for a large Wall Street firm is very difficult and very prestigious. It is also very lucrative. *Institutional Investor* All-American's analysts routinely take home US$1 million per year in compensation. Former superstar analysts like Morgan Stanley's internet guru Mary Meeker and Salomon's telecom analyst Jack Grubman earned an estimated US$15 million per year. When you are compensated this well, a major motivating factor in your work is to keep your wonderful, high paying job. This factor alone can clearly explain why sell recommendations historically are less than 2%, although this is starting to change. A company whose stock has been rated a sell by an analyst at a brokerage firm is not likely to send investment banking business to that firm. So they won't issue a sell unless they are willing to risk not getting banking business from a company.

This behavior can lead to some rather embarrassing fiascos, such as the internet collapse, when analysts were still making buy recommendations as the internet stocks were crashing, and, more recently, Enron. After the announcement on 16 October 2001 by Enron CEO Ken Lay that the company would lose US$1.2 billion in shareholder equity, the Prudential Securities analyst for the stock wrote that she was 'dismayed' but kept a buy rating on the stock, and did not reduce her target price, which was US$55. Enron was trading at US$33 at the time. The Lehman Brothers analyst told clients to 'rustle up a little courage' and maintained a strong buy rating on the stock. The reason for the strong support of Enron was that is was a huge generator of fees for many investment banking firms, doing 41 merger and acquisition transactions in a period of less then two and a half years.

Analysts may not want to issue sell recommendations, but can't they be more accurate? When you have any high profile job, the best way to keep it is to not make any large errors. When an analyst is far away from the consensus and right, they won't get any more reward than when they are near the consensus and correct. However, if the analyst is far away from the consensus and wrong, he or she risks losing their job.

Analyst information flow

Regulation FD took effect in 2000. Reg FD requires companies to release new information in a public manner, not just privately to Wall Street firms. This new regulation helped continue to regulate information flow and keep analyst estimates useful. During the tech bubble in 1998 and 1999, a growing phenomenon had been whisper estimates. Whisper estimates are unofficial forecasts of earnings per share that are used by investors. During the bubble, investors were keen on any whisper numbers they could get. At least three web sites cropped up to supply this almost insatiable need.

Academic studies by Bagnoli, Beneish, and Watts (1999) compared whisper estimates collected from web chat rooms to the First Call consensus. They found that the whisper estimates were closer to the reported earnings per share on average, and did not have the same understated bias as the First Call consensus. In light of the evidence that corporations are managing forecasts to small positive surprises, this does not seem like an unreasonable finding.

With the popping of the tech bubble and the onset of Reg FD, whisper estimates began to fade. According to Edmonston (2001), whisper estimates were reported in news stories in 2001 one tenth of the times they had been in the year 2000. Whispers became popular in 1999 and 2000 due to a desire by day traders for the latest information. Day trading required moving in and out of stocks faster than analysts would publish information about the securities, hence the unofficial estimates known as whispers.

Whispers were supposed to be coming from analysts on a frequent basis and sent to their best clients before they were published. When Reg FD came into effect, it barred companies from selectively disclosing key information to their favorite analyst, and that analyst from selectively disclosing information to his/her key clients. This limited the key sources of whispers. Getwhispers.com has seen a 'definite drop in interest', while WhisperNumbers.com continues to scrape chat rooms for information, and claims that investors are still interested in the numbers. It is unlikely that whispers will ever have the prominence and cachet that they once had.

The changing nature of analyst estimates

Over the years, it has been the job of CFOs of major corporations to tweak the books in order to make earnings appear more stable than they really are. They did this because they believed that investors would reward them for predictability. Then came the internet mania, and CFOs stretched the envelope even further in trying to show good results to investors.

So how do companies smooth out their earnings? Firms that issue credit can report higher earnings by adjusting their default rates on loans to levels that are too low to push up earnings. The default rate can be pushed up later, when the company is doing better, to bring earnings down. These actions in combination create a smoothed earnings pattern. A company can push product out to dealers and distributors, and book the revenue, even if the merchandise can be returned at a later date, bringing profits up. Later, when revenues are better, the returns can be booked.

All of the above manipulations can occur within Generally Accepted Accounting Principles (GAAP). These are the numbers created by a firm's auditors, and reported to the Securities and Exchange Commission. The 1990s, however, popularized a new set of earnings numbers, the pro forma earnings. These numbers are not regulated like GAAP earnings, and allow firms to exclude such basic costs as marketing and interest. One famous pro forma story is about a firm who repainted their fleet of vehicles on a regular schedule. After deciding to paint the vehicles before their schedule date, the firm excluded the cost of painting, claiming that since it wasn't scheduled it was an extraordinary item, and should not be included as an expense in their pro forma earnings numbers.

Pro forma has become such a fixture in the press that it was the subject of a column by Rob Walker on cnbc.com. An excerpt is illuminating:

> PRO FORMA literally means 'for the sake of form,' but the *Wall Street Journal* sheds light on what the phrase means to corporations in America when it explains that 'a growing number present their earnings on a "pro forma" basis, "as if" certain expenses didn't exist.' This is not a scandalous idea; it's a delightful one.
>
> On a pro forma basis, I'm having an outstanding year. In calendar 2002 I've gone to the gym on a regular basis and expect this trend to continue and to have a material impact on my health going forward. Year-to-date, my health has improved by a solid 15 percent on an annualized basis.
>
> These results do not reflect certain items. Loss of good health and potential mortality stemming from 62 consecutive quarters of above-plan intake of assorted spirits, tobacco, and other substances reliant on mouth-to-lung delivery systems, and miscellaneous off-book chemical and pharmaceutical substances, are addressed in a one-time write-down. Results also include the application of 'good will' regarding those days, and in some cases weeks, when actual gym attendance was negatively impacted or curtailed by visits to the racetrack, where I ate oysters and drank Budweiser. Finally, a recent post-workout lunch of a 22-ounce, bone-in rib steak at Smith & Wollensky and three shots of bourbon is treated here as a non-recurring expense. I'll never do

that again! I encourage you to focus on these pro forma results as a truer portrait of the state of my health than 'traditional measures,' which suggest that I have been dead for at least a year.[1]

The problems with pro forma earnings have led the SEC to issue a warning to companies to stop using pro forma earnings. Pro forma earnings 'can make it hard for investors to compare an issuer's financial information with other reporting periods and with other companies', the SEC wrote. The SEC warned investors to be especially careful looking at reports that contain alternative calculations of financial results, leave out non-recurring transactions, and vary widely from GAAP results.

Effect of pro forma versus GAAP earnings on the investor

The current gap between pro forma and GAAP earnings is the widest in history. In fact, Standard & Poor's and First Call, both using pro forma earnings, still estimated that earnings fell by 32% versus 17% in 2001, based mainly on how special items were treated. This caused a valuation difference that is significant. In looking at the price/earnings ratio of the S&P 500, it was approximately 36 using GAAP earnings, 24 using S&P earnings, and 22 using First Call earnings. Looking at Exhibit 3.3, you can see how clearly the gap has widened between GAAP and pro forma earnings for the S&P 500.

An exhaustive report on the subject by Keon (2001) looked at the differences. First, he found that a key difference was whether the ratio was calculated based on trailing or estimated earnings. Another difference was the way pro forma earnings were calculated.

Reported earnings 'could be whatever the company could convince analysts were correct', according to Keon, a former executive at I/B/E/S. He speculates that when the gaps began they were driven by two changes in corporate practices: the merger and acquisition boom, and the re-structuring movement. Many companies, due to a need to show the results from an acquisition or to deal with poor performance, discontinued, sold or cut back on mar-

Exhibit 3.3

Differences in GAAP and pro forma earnings

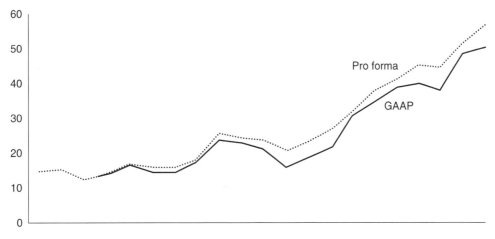

Source: Authors' own.

ginal operations, thereby taking a one time charge against earnings. By the 1990s, companies like General Motors were taking charges due to how pension liabilities were accounted for. Since this was no change in the actual liability, companies excluded these charges from earnings. By the late 1990s, internet firms had taken this practice to extremes, excluding marketing costs, shipping costs and other normal expenses associated with doing business.

This has caused investors to push analysts to take a deeper look at pro forma earnings. Merrill Lynch in early 2002 told its analysts to use a variety of methods to judge financial performance rather than relying on pro forma earnings when reporting on a company. In an internal memo, Merrill is adopting in its research 'the use of broad measures beyond pro forma earnings to evaluate a company's quality of earnings with the objective of establishing an enhanced standard of accountability and transparency for our clients'. The goal is to use the tougher GAAP standards more rigorously in evaluating firms.

Earnings forecast quality

How good are earnings forecasts? Much work has been done by academics on the accuracy of estimates. Work by David Dreman (1988) in Exhibit 3.4 suggests errors of up to 41%.

Five year growth rates are also notorious for their lack of quality. It has been very noticeable recently in the technology sector. It was very typical in late 2001 to see companies with growth rates based on consensus estimates to be negative for the next three years, but to have the five year growth rate of earnings at 25% per year or higher, which were similar growth rates to those projected for those firms in 1998 and 1999. Merrill Lynch calculated a bottom up five year projected earnings growth rate for the S&P 500, and found it to be 17.4% in early 2001. This compared to a high during the tech bubble of 18.7% and an average since 1980 of 12.8%. The same growth rate calculated for the technology sector was 26.7%. The highest projection during the bubble was 28%, and the average since 1980 was 17.3%. This evidence clearly suggests that five-year growth rate numbers are not accurate. This could be for a

Exhibit 3.4

Forecast error as a percentage of reported earnings, 1973–2000

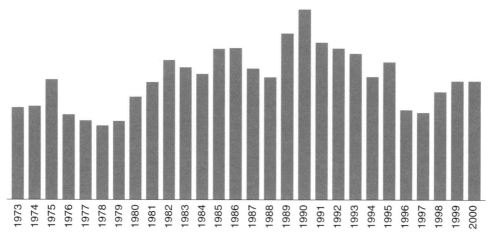

Source: David Dreman.

number of reasons. The most likely is that they are not updated very frequently, and are much harder to project due to their long term nature.

Summary

Analysts form a critical link in the information cycle. Companies and portfolio managers need someone to function as a repository and filter of information. Analysts have strong incentives to herd their results close to other analysts, but not as many incentives to be accurate. From the Dreman study above, accuracy has never been very good. If a portfolio manager is using earnings estimates to create a discounted earnings valuation of a firm, this flawed data will create incredibly bad estimates of value. If, however, a portfolio manager realizes how inaccurate the data is, they can craft strategies that utilize the information in the data while compensating for the inaccuracy. Subsequent chapters in this book look at tools like earnings revision and earnings surprise which are useful even with less than perfect data.

References

Angwin, Julia, and Martin Peers (2001), 'Cold Calls: AOL May Be Snubbing Merrill', *Wall Street Journal,* 1 November.

Bagnoli, Mark, Daniel Beneish, and Susan Watts (1999), 'Whisper Forecasts of Quarterly Earnings Per Share', *Journal of Accounting and Economics,* November.

Bernstein, Richard (2001), 'Five-Year Growth Rates Haven't Budged', *Merrill Lynch Quantitative Strategy Update,* 16 January.

Dreman, David (1998), *Contrarian Investment Strategies: The Next Generation,* Simon and Schuster.

Edmonston, Peter (2001), 'Focus on Whisper Numbers Fades As Pundits Sidestep the Informal Targets', *Wall Street Journal,* 26 July.

Keon, Ed (2001), 'What's the P/E Ratio of the S&P 500?', *Prudential Equity Research,* 29 October.

Lauricella, Tom (2001), 'Analyst Reports Pressures of Employer's Trading', *Wall Street Journal,* 4 September.

Li, Xi (2002), 'Career Concerns of Analysts: Compensation, Termination and Performance', Vanderbilt University Working Paper.

Williams, Neil (2002), 'The Quality and Quantity of Earnings: Both are Cyclical', *Goldman Sachs Global Portfolio Strategy,* 21 February.

---

[1] Walker, Rob (2002), 'My Pro Forma Life', 2 April, www.cnbc.com.

[2] *Source:* Marketing materials produced by David Dreman. Reproduced with permission.

Chapter 4

Analysts' conflicts of interest

Analysts are whores.

Stanley Bing

As discussed previously, sell side analysts are a source of a number of primary pieces of information relevant to those wishing to effectively invest in common stocks. The analysts provide projections of earnings growth, purchase recommendations, target prices, and commentary on the possible risks and rewards of owning a particular stock. These research analysts are supposed to be filters between the companies they follow and the investors that they serve. These analysts are also providing a critical link in the information flow between company and investor. However, these analysts work for investment firms that are paid huge sums of money to finance deals for the same companies covered by the analysts. How much faith should be placed in the research reports and recommendations of analysts, given that they are essentially paid by the firms they are evaluating? Maybe it is as some market observers have noted, that everyone knows about the conflicts of interest except those who do not.

A study by Investars.com tracked the profitability of brokerage recommendations and found that, relative to a sample period S&P 500 return of 75%, the best brokerage house released recommendations over the same period that would have earned just under 8%. One columnist for Smart Money stated that this is 'a breathtaking level of underperformance that should have every client who follows such research flocking to an index fund.'

In light of results such as those reported by Investars.com, the credibility of analysts' research has been called into question in the financial press because of seemingly perverse conflicts of interest that face sell side analysts. Scrutiny on analysts has intensified in recent years. In 2001, the U.S. Congress held hearings related to this issue. Moreover, the Securities Industry Association has formalized a list of best practices related to the sell side analyst function.

Much has been made of the impact of analysts' conflicts of interest by means of several anecdotal cases. However, is there any evidence of systematic problems driven by analysts' conflicts of interest? In this chapter, the evidence is reviewed.

A brief history

The large investment banks originally employed research analysts to specialize and provide analyses of various companies. The analysts' outputs, primarily research reports, were then marketed to various clients of the investment bank. These clients were typically large buy side analysts, institutional investors, and wealth managers. The analysts were compensated based on their ability to produce high quality research that was useful to the bank's clients.

Just several decades ago, the typical brokerage firm received well over half of its revenue from commissions on stock transactions executed by its customers. However, this all

Exhibit 4.1

Distribution of recommendations

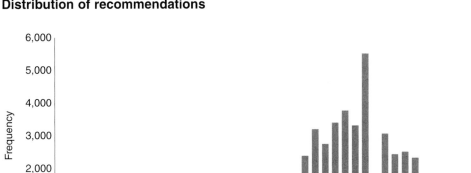

Source: Bradshaw (2000).

changed in May 1975 (often referred to as 'May Day'), when commissions were deregulated. This fundamentally changed the landscape of the research analyst function by deregulating the fees charged to investors for executing trades, which ushered in competition. The new competition for clients ensued, and investors realized an overall decline in commission fees. As part of the competition, many banks began 'giving away' their analysts' earnings forecasts, recommendations, and even entire research reports as a means of attracting and retaining clients. As a result, the income structure of the investment banks was altered such that trading commissions and research revenue were displaced by investment banking fees.

Soon thereafter, investment banking fees displaced commission fees as the primary source of revenue, and provided the brokerages with a new means of financial support. As a consequence, skeptics have claimed that analysts' earnings forecasts, stock recommendations, and target prices are all optimistically biased, serving no purpose other than marketing stocks to investors and maintaining happy relations with managers of companies that access the capital markets. The most frequently cited example is the fact that there are virtually no sell recommendations (see Exhibit 4.1).

This figure presents the distribution of the mean consensus stock recommendations for the years 1994–98, and reflects 46,222 observations. There are no strong sell recommendations and very few consensus recommendations below the level of hold (less than 1%). Clearly, the distribution is shifted to the right (optimism), which is consistent with rampant optimistic bias in recommendations. For this reason, many investors essentially view hold recommendations as sell recommendations. The optimism in stock recommendations extends to target prices as well, as seen in Exhibit 4.2.

For 52,318 target prices issued during 1997–99, the figure plots the distribution of the ratio TP/P, where TP is an analyst's 12-month target price scaled by the actual trad-

Exhibit 4.2

Target price/price

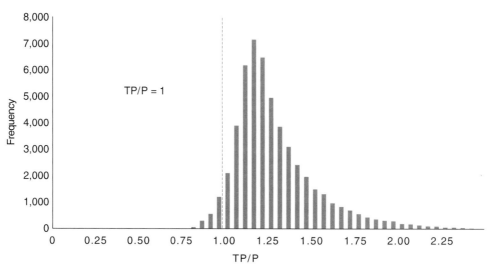

Source: Bradshaw and Brown (2002).

ing price just before the release of the target price. Clearly, there is optimistic bias in the target prices similar to that for recommendations. There are very few target prices (less than 2%) where the TP/P ratio is less than one (which implies a predicted decline in stock price).

However, another possibility is plausible, and consistent with anecdotal and academic evidence. The alternative is that when analysts have sufficiently negative views on a company's earnings prospects, its valuation, or other aspect of the company, then the analyst simply does not report those opinions. This is akin to the adage, 'If you don't have anything nice to say, then don't say anything at all.' If analysts behave in this manner, then we would see a truncation of 'bad news.' For instance, in frequency distributions of stock recommendations and target prices, we would expect to see the distributions noted above because analysts don't release negative recommendations or target prices. Academic research has shown other evidence consistent with this. For example, most of the time when an analyst initiates coverage on a stock, she does so with a 'buy' rating. Similarly, downgrades of stock recommendations are infrequent and, when they occur, are delayed relative to the time elapsing prior to upgrades. Moreover, analysts' initial ratings on stocks seem to be a prelude to higher return on equity for such stocks than for previously covered stocks and stocks that are subsequently dropped from coverage, suggesting that the initial optimism reflects fundamentals, as opposed to an attempt to appease management.

What are the conflicts?

Who are analysts' clients? The firms they cover, the institutional investors that are the largest consumers of their research, or the retail investors who obtain summary figures off free internet sites?

The most talked about conflict of interest facing analysts is related to the large investment banking fees that support the big Wall Street firms. It is common for analysts to have a large portion of their compensation related to their support of the investment banking operations in obtaining lucrative corporate finance deals. However, these analysts are also charged with providing objective research that is useful to the buy side clients. There is a conflict to the extent that an individual analyst derives compensation related to efforts to attract investment banking clients, which reportedly is related to the favorableness of research reports released. The impact of this conflict on the analyst's actual behavior is mitigated by the reputation effect associated with providing high quality research reports to the buy side.

Although the investment banking conflict is the most frequently cited conflict, analysts are subject to a number of additional conflicts.

Themselves – rose colored glasses

Within limits, analysts have some freedom in their ability to choose what companies to follow. It should not be surprising that, as analysts settle into an equilibrium in their coverage of stocks, and as they learn more about the companies they follow, they might 'fall in love' with certain companies. Thus, we primarily see analysts reporting on stocks that they favor, not those that they dislike and have chosen not to cover. This is consistent with the self selection story discussed above.

Themselves – analyst compensation structure

Analysts readily admit that companies communicate with them much more freely when an analyst has issued a good recommendation on their stock. This type of reward and punishment behavior by companies has a strong effect on analysts. So why do they care so much? The answer is analyst compensation.

Becoming an analyst for a large Wall Street firm is very difficult and very prestigious. It is also very lucrative. *Institutional Investor* All-American analysts routinely take home US$1 million per year in compensation. Superstar analysts like Morgan Stanley's internet guru Mary Meeker and Salomon telecom analyst Jack Grubman earn an estimated US$15 million per year. When you are compensated this well, a major motivating factor in your work is to keep your wonderful, high paying job. This factor alone can clearly explain why sell recommendations are less than 2%.

This behavior can lead to some rather embarrassing fiascos, such as the internet collapse, when analyst were still making buy recommendations as the internet stocks were crashing, and, more recently, in other companies such as Enron. After the announcement on 16 October 2001 by Enron CEO Ken Lay that the company would lose US$1.2 billion in shareholder equity, the Prudential Securities analyst for the stock wrote that she was 'dismayed' but kept a buy rating on the stock, and did not reduce her target price, which was US$55. Enron was trading at US$33 at the time. The Lehman Brothers analyst told clients to 'rustle up a little courage' and maintained a strong buy rating on the stock. The reason for the strong support of Enron may have been at least partially attributable to the fact that it was a huge generator of fees for many investment banking firms, doing 41 merger and acquisition transactions in a period of less than two and a half years.

Themselves – owning stocks in firms covered

Very few brokerages place restrictions on stocks that analysts can own. Thus, analysts often have a personal financial stake in the companies that they cover. The resulting conflict is clear. However, a counter argument is that analysts should own stocks that they cover, to 'put their money where their mouth is.' A countervailing force, as with the investment banking conflict, is that analysts also value their reputations, which mitigates the impact of the personal financial wealth invested in any single company.

Themselves – holding positions opposite to those promoted

There is anecdotal evidence of analysts taking personal financial positions in stocks that are opposite those recommended in their reports. This would occur if an analyst is unloading stock for which she has an outstanding strong buy recommendation. Even more egregious, there have been reports of analysts who actually short stocks for which their reports contain buy recommendations.

Management

Much of the information obtained by analysts comes from management directly. It is widely accepted that analysts are afraid of saying something too negative about a company because management will likely blackball them. Why might this be? If they did utter something less than favorable, they may alienate a client of their firm and risk future investment banking business. Or they may simply be cut off from information flow from a firm. For example, one well publicized account was that of Roger Lipton, who issued a sell recommendation on Boston Chicken (before it filed for Chapter 11), and, as a result, was excluded from subsequent analysts' meetings with the company's management team.

Moreover, thanks to extensive use of stock option compensation plans, managers typically have a large stake in the share prices of their own firms. Accordingly, managers tend to pressure analysts to maintain an optimistic report on the company, so that the stock price is maintained or increased, and management benefits through option exercises.

Another example is when investment banking firms try to utilize analysts as marketers, as in the Bear Sterns example from the chapter 'Role of analysts'.

Institutional investors

An often overlooked source of pressure on analysts' objectivity is the investment firm's large institutional investor clients. Much of the benefit of serving the institutional investors comes through 'soft dollar' arrangements, in which the institutional client gets free or very low cost research in exchange for an agreement to execute a certain number of transactions or level of trading with the investment firm. Although the buy side often does their own research, they still incorporate sell side research as part of their own research. However, another reason the institutional clients are interested in the research reports of the sell side is that they know that research affects security prices. An institutional investor would be extremely unhappy if they have a large position in a stock that receives a negative research report from an analyst that sends the stock falling. 'Don't put a sell on this stock because it will ruin my fund's performance!' Thus, this is another source of pressure on analysts who would otherwise release purely unbiased research.

Academic evidence

Given the attention that analysts' presumed conflicts of interest receive in the financial press, the number of academic studies investigating the conflicts is surprisingly small. Perhaps academics, like the financial press, believe that it is a foregone conclusion that analysts are indeed subject to conflicts of interest, and believe the topic to have been settled by the few studies that exist.

In examining whether analysts are subject to conflicts of interest, one would naturally look at analysts' primary outputs (earnings forecasts and recommendations), which is exactly what researchers have done. The first issue that has to be tackled in examining whether an analyst colors their outputs with bias is how to measure 'conflict.' Clearly, an analyst working for an investment firm that is the lead underwriter for a stock covered by the analyst is a candidate for study. However, at what point in time? Suppose analyst X worked for investment firm Y, and investment firm Y managed a securities offering for company Z in 1999. Would analyst X feel the pressures on her to say positive things before this securities offering in 1999? After the offering? How long before and after a securities offering should the researcher assume that the analyst was subject to pressure from a conflict of interest? What about analyst Y, who works at a brokerage house that did not participate in the 1999 securities offering? Can we safely assume that analyst Y is free from pressures to bias their reports, or is it possible that analyst Y's brokerage house is vying for the next securities offering from company Z? These are non-trivial issues when attempting to measure something as obscure as a 'conflict of interest.'

In addition to the direct relation between an analyst's brokerage house and a company being covered, recall the other conflicts mentioned earlier related to (i) an analyst's own views and personal holdings in the covered company, (ii) management, (iii) institutional investor clients with large stakes in companies covered by the analyst. Unfortunately, data on these other sources of conflicts are difficult, if not impossible, to obtain. Thus, existing research is restricted to examining conflicts arising from underwriting relationships between an analyst's employer and a covered company.

One way to measure an investment banking relationship is to access America's Corporate Finance Directory (formerly the Corporate Finance Bluebook). This publication lists data for large U.S. public (and private) companies with assets or revenues in excess of US$100 million. An early study examined forecasts and recommendations from analysts employed by brokerages identified as a company's primary investment banker. With a goal of measuring 'bias' in an investment banker analyst's forecasts or recommendations, a benchmark is needed, which can be forecasts and recommendations of a non-investment banker analyst following the same company. The early study found that investment banker analysts do indeed provide more optimistic earnings forecasts than their non-investment banker counterparts, although the differences were not 'statistically significant.' Additionally, the investment banker analysts reported more favorable recommendations, on average.

An alternative way to examine for evidence of a conflict of interest impact on analysts' forecasts and recommendations is to isolate a specific event, such as an initial public or seasoned equity offering. Then, you can identify the analysts affiliated with a company, and examine whether their forecasts and recommendations are indeed more optimistic than those of analysts not affiliated with the company. The existence of a specific event increases the chance that a researcher is looking at a time and relationship where there might be the strongest evidence of a conflict of interest.

When a company issues securities as part of an initial public offering or a seasoned equity offering, there are generally two classes of investment firms. Typically, the entire process is managed by a 'lead' manager, who coordinates the regulatory filings and required due diligence work. In addition, there are typically other brokerage houses involved in secondary roles, collectively known as the 'syndicate'. Since the lead manager has the most to gain or lose relative to a specific securities offering (such as over or under-allocated shares, legal liability, and the like), it is reasonable to expect that analysts working for the lead manager brokerage would be the most susceptible to the effects of a conflict of interest. As a result, several studies examine differential bias in forecasts and recommendations for both classes of affiliated analysts separately.

Identifying analysts as affiliated or unaffiliated is the difficult aspect of studying for a conflict of interest around a securities offering. Once identified, you may simply measure the average level of earnings forecasts or stock recommendations for affiliated analysts, and compare them to those of unaffiliated analysts. A benefit of focusing on a specific event is that you can examine changes over time in any observed levels of optimism. Presumably, affiliated analysts, especially those from the lead manager brokerages, will tend to be most optimistic just around a securities offering. Exhibit 4.3 presents the average stock recommendation for lead underwriter analysts relative to unaffiliated analysts around the time of a seasoned equity offering.

The bold line represents the average recommendation of lead underwriter analysts from 36 days before to 36 days after a seasoned equity offering. The other line represents the aver-

Exhibit 4.3

Effect of underwriting on recommendations

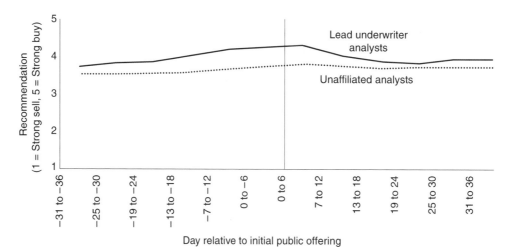

Source: Figure constructed from data tabulated in Lin and McNichols (1998), Table 3.

age recommendation of unaffiliated analysts over the same time frame. More favorable recommendations are reflected in the figure higher on the y-axis. Two things are clear from the figure. First, lead underwriter analysts increase the favorableness before and around the time of an equity offering. Second, lead underwriter analysts have an overall higher level of optimism than unaffiliated analysts. The differences are statistically significant.

Most published academic studies that examine bias stemming from analysts' conflicts of interest demonstrate that affiliated analysts issue more favorable recommendations. However, those studies find mixed evidence regarding whether earnings forecasts are significantly higher for the affiliated analysts. This should not be surprising, for a number of reasons. First, companies announce earnings every quarter, and the earnings announcements season on Wall Street is a closely watched ritual. Analysts have reputations and compensation that are at least partially affected by their abilities to forecast earnings accurately. For example, *Institutional Investor* and the *Wall Street Journal* both compile rankings of analysts that are based in part on the analyst's track record of earnings forecasting accuracy. To the extent that the analyst cares about these rankings, this mitigates any incentives to optimistically bias the earnings forecasts. Second, neither managers nor investors like to see earnings announcements that fall short of earnings expectations. Thus, even if analysts cared nothing about earnings forecast accuracy for their own reputation or compensation, they probably do care about keeping management happy. As such, this also works against overly optimistic earnings forecasts.

Recommendations, on the other hand, are discrete, and have an ambiguous time horizon. Although it is possible to check on the profitability of an analyst's portfolio of recommendations, you need to make a number of assumptions regarding portfolio turnover, reinvestment of dividends, and the like. Thus, an analyst has more 'degrees of freedom' with a recommendation than an earnings forecast, and would be more likely to infuse desired optimistic bias into recommendations as opposed to earnings forecasts, consistent with the evidence.

Movements towards combating conflicts of interest

Declines in stock prices that began near the end of 1999 have brought with them the inevitable calls for accountability. Analysts that became celebrities in the roaring bull market that began that decade were turned into pariahs. Accordingly, there have been congressional hearings on the matter, and various rule changes have been proposed by the National Association of Securities Dealers, Inc. (NASD), and the New York Stock Exchange (NYSE). Both of these organizations are classified by the Securities and Exchange Commission as 'self-regulatory organizations', and their proposals are an attempt to retain the self-regulatory stature of their respective organizations.

The proposals set forth by the NASD and NYSE set a number of new specific rules that restrict the nature and behavior of sell side analysts. The rules are somewhat detailed, and have collectively been referred to by some as the 'Fair Employment for Lawyers Act.' The proposed rules have been met by the predictable disapproval of those directly affected – the investment firms. Some representatives from the investment firms have chided that the rules should actually be named the 'Full Employment for Lumberjacks Act' because of an expected increase in documentation required under the rules.

NASD Rule 2711 ('Research Analysts and Research Reports') specifies, among other things, several general guidelines.

- No research analyst may be subject to the supervision or control of any employee of the member's investment banking department.
- No employee of the investment banking department may review or approve a research report of a research analyst before its publication.
- No research analyst may submit a research report to the subject company before its publication.
- No research analyst may receive compensation that is based on a specific investment banking services transaction.
- No research analyst may offer favorable research as consideration for the receipt of business or compensation.
- No research analyst may purchase or receive securities of companies engaged in similar types of business as the companies the research analyst follows.
- No research analyst may purchase or sell any security in a manner inconsistent with the research analyst's recommendation.
- A research analyst must disclose in research reports and/or public appearances a number of items related to:

  - personal financial interests;
  - relevant investment banking revenues;
  - meanings of stock ratings;
  - distribution of all ratings issued;
  - historical stock price charts with the analyst's ratings or price targets; and
  - market making activities.

The list above intentionally excluded certain legal jargon, and hence does not include a multitude of exceptions and additional details. NYSE Rule 472 ('Communications with the Public') lists similar rules, and also incorporates a number of guidelines related to public appearances through the media, books, magazines, and newspapers.

Currently, most brokerages have a boiler-plate disclaimer to the effect that 'the investment firm and/or its employees may have an interest in the securities described'. The proposed rules would require more specific disclosures that varied across each report. Additionally, some of the required disclosures would require the investment firms to tabulate a large volume of data in research reports that essentially amount to the analyst giving herself a 'report card' on past research. Perhaps some of the more contentious issues addressed in the rules are those related to disclosures regarding fees paid by companies to investment firms. Specifically, certain rules mandate the disclosure of fees paid by the subject company 'within twelve months before' the publication of the research report or the fees that the investment firm 'reasonably expects to receive . . . within three months following publication of the research report'. Disclosure of future fees is argued to put undue burdens on proprietary information regarding future transactions that the company might be contemplating (for example, takeovers).

In 2001, the Securities Industry Association (SIA) adopted a set of 'best practices' that more or less mimicked the primary points listed in the NASD and NYSE rules, albeit somewhat watered down, causing some to worry that the best practices would result in no changes. Indeed, a number of spokespersons for the large investment firms publicly stated that the SIA best practices would not necessitate any changes to their current practices.

Summary

In the modern work of fiction *Half Asleep in Frog Pajamas*, Tom Robbins states:

> [I]t's common knowledge that brokers push stocks and other instruments based on what the brokerage firm wants to peddle on a given day or week. It's also common knowledge that unsuspecting customers are sold specific securities (mutual funds are a good example) that result in the highest commission for the broker. It's a fact of life, sad but true, that most brokers have their own interests at the forefront of every buy and sell recommendation that they proffer. That just goes with the territory, I guess.

Ironically, the sentiment echoed by Tom Robbins the satirist seems to permeate the market. One of the greatest assets inherent in the U.S. capital markets is the amount of credibility and trust that characterize them. Recent events surrounding the decline in the Nasdaq and the 'bursting of the dot.com bubble' have shaken this credibility. If investors in the United States or elsewhere perceive a decline in the credibility of the U.S. markets as indicative of a 'rigged game', then everyone stands to lose (investors, companies, analysts, governments, and labor). Regulators are reacting to perceived abuses by participants in the capital markets in order to restore this asset.

References

Bing, Stanley (2002), 'Lessons from the Abyss', *Fortune*, 18 February, p. 49.

For a nice conversational explanation of the conflicts of interest facing analysts, see the testimony before the U.S. House Committee on Financial Services on 31 July 2001 by Charles L. Hill, Director of Financial Research at Thomson Financial/First Call.

The graph of recommendations is taken from:

Bradshaw, M.T. (2000), 'The Articulation of Sell-Side Analysts' Earnings Forecasts, Common Stock Valuations, and Investment Recommendations,' Dissertation, University of Michigan.

Lauricella, Tom (2001), 'Analyst Reports Pressures of Employer's Trading', *Wall Street Journal*, 4 September.

The paper that is consistent with bad news being truncated from analysts' research is:

McNichols, M., and P.C. O'Brien (1997), 'Self-Selection and Analyst Coverage,' *Journal of Accounting Research*, Supplement, pp. 167–199.

The following are the seminal research papers addressing the impact of analysts' conflicts of interest on their earnings forecasts and stock recommendations:

Dechow, P., A. Hutton, and R. Sloan (2000), 'The Relation between Analysts' Long-Term Earnings Forecasts and Stock Performance Following Equity Offerings', *Contemporary Accounting Research,* Vol. 17, No. 3.

Dugar, A., and S. Nathan (1995), 'The Effects of Investment Banking Relationships on Financial Analysts' Earnings Forecasts and Investment Recommendations', *Contemporary Accounting Research,* Vol. 12, pp. 131–160.

Lin, H., and M.F. McNichols (1998), 'Underwriting Relationships, Analysts' Earnings Forecasts and Investment Recommendations', *Journal of Accounting and Economics, Vol.* 25, pp. 101–127.

Michaely, R., and K.L. Womack (1999), 'Conflict of Interest and the Credibility of Underwriter Analyst Recommendations', *The Review of Financial Studies*, Vol. 12, No. 4, pp. 653–686.

Robbins, Tom (1994), *Half Asleep in Frog Pajamas*, London, No Exit Press.

Chapter 5

Forecasts of long-term earnings growth, target prices, and stock recommendations

Creation comes before distribution – or there will be nothing to distribute.

Ayn Rand

The emphasis in this book is on earnings forecasts, the data most commonly available from analysts and the data that has been collected for the longest. However, earnings forecasts are but one of many forecasted data items now available. In addition to forecasts of earnings over the next few quarters or years, analysts consistently provide three additional items, and are starting to provide even more. First, they forecast the level of earnings growth over longer term horizons. Second, they provide target prices, which are forecasts of actual price levels. Finally, they issue stock recommendations to buy or sell securities. Moving forward, they are starting to estimate sales and other income statement information that may be less likely to be involved in the GAAP versus pro forma earnings discussion (which is covered in a later chapter). In this chapter, these other items are considered, and we discuss how useful these metrics are to investor stock selection models.

Long-term earnings growth

Most firms expect, or at least hope, that they will realize growth in earnings levels over longer time horizons. However, the majority of the earnings related focus in the stock markets seems to be placed on the quarterly earnings announcement season. Thus, one of the primary focal points of investors and traders during a firm's fiscal year is the upcoming quarterly earnings announcement.

For any given fiscal year, there are three quarterly earnings announcements plus a fourth announcement, which covers the year. By virtue of the first three quarterly announcements, the annual earnings announcement is for all intents and purposes just another quarterly earnings announcement (see Exhibit 5.1).

Thus, at any particular point in time, investors can probably obtain data on forecasts of earnings for at least the next two quarters, and probably the next four. Moreover, they can

Exhibit 5.1

T1 minimum of announcements

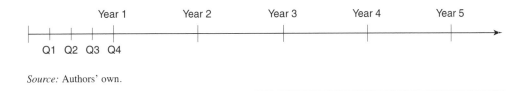

Source: Authors' own.

31

most likely find forecasts for the current and next fiscal year. Analysts sometimes forecast earnings beyond this horizon, but such forecasts are not as common.

Instead of forecasting the actual level of earnings over periods farther out than two years, analysts tend to provide a forecast of the level of earnings growth. Deemed forecasts of 'long-term' earnings growth, such forecasts are generally understood to be forecasts covering earnings growth within the three to five year forecast horizon. An elementary understanding of valuation theory indicates that expectations covering levels of earnings and cash flows over longer horizons have a significant impact on current valuations. On the flip side, however, this also means that errors or bias in such forecasts also have a significant impact on current valuations.

Dechow and Sloan (1997) examined the long-term growth forecasts available between 1981 and 1993. Exhibit 5.2 is based on data reported in their study.

Exhibit 5.2 shows average forecasted earnings growth and the realized earnings growth across deciles, based on the level of forecasted earnings growth. Although there is a positive correlation between the forecasted and realized levels of growth, it appears that the realized levels of earnings growth are less than half of the forecasted levels, on average.

Since the forecast horizons are longer, we expect that the precision of such forecasts would be lower than the precision of nearer term forecasts, such as earnings at a one year horizon. However, it is puzzling why the error would be asymmetric, with analysts consistently overestimating the levels of future earnings growth. One possibility is that the analysts that generally provide forecasts of earnings growth are those that have current or prospective investment banking relationships with the company being forecasted. However, given the frequency with which these forecasts are provided, it is unlikely that this explanation explains the entire phenomenon.

Thus, it appears that the forecasts of long-term earnings growth are not very reliable on average. However, it turns out that such forecasts are useful anyway. As Dechow and Sloan show in their study, it appears that the over optimistic forecasts of earnings growth are impounded in

Exhibit 5.2

Forecasted versus actual long-term growth, 1981–93

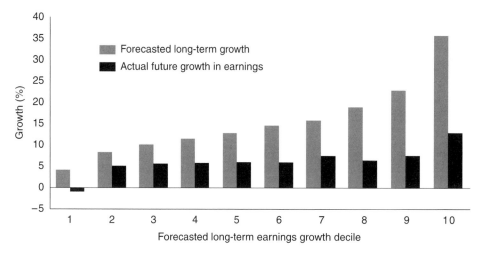

Source: Deschow and Sloan (1977).

stock prices. Since higher expected levels of growth have a disproportionate impact on stock prices, analysts' forecasts of growth are actually a contrarian indicator of future stock returns. In fact, Dechow and Sloan attempt to quantify how much of the returns to several contrarian investment strategies is captured by the forecasted long-term earnings growth factor (for example, the book-to-market, earnings-to-price, and cash-to-price strategies). They state that 'earnings tend to grow at less than half the rate predicted by analysts, but that stock prices initially reflect substantially all of the forecast earnings growth. Finally, we show that investors' naïve reliance on analysts' growth forecasts explains over half of the returns to contrarian strategies'.

Overall, the usefulness of analysts' long-term earnings growth forecasts appears limited. However, as will be discussed later, analysts' other outputs (target prices and stock recommendations) seem to significantly rely on the forecasted long-term earnings growth numbers.

Stock recommendations

Of the three non earnings outputs, the general investor or market observer is most familiar with stock recommendations. The presumption underlying a stock recommendation is that it indicates stocks that are either overvalued (sell), fairly valued (hold), or undervalued (buy). However, the virtual non existence of sell recommendations is well known. For example, the median consensus stock recommendations issued between 1994 and 1998 are distributed as follows (see Exhibit 5.3).

Clearly, analysts are not fond of releasing sell recommendations. One explanation is that analysts are biased because of their conflicts of interest. However, another reason we see fewer sell recommendations is offered by McNichols and O'Brien (1997), who argue and show evidence consistent with analysts adopting an 'If you don't have anything nice to say, don't say anything at all' policy. Thus, the absence of sell recommendations is simply due to the fact that analysts refrain from issuing such recommendations or drop coverage of a firm rather than releasing an explicit recommendation to sell.

Exhibit 5.3

Distribution of stock recommendations, 1994–98

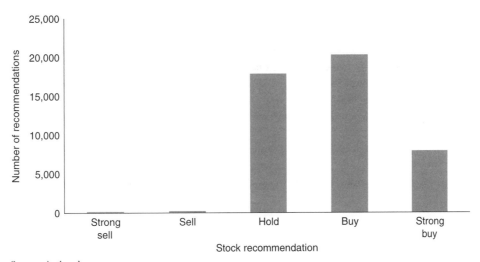

Source: Authors' own.

Conventional wisdom, however, assumes that analysts do issue sell recommendations, but it is understood that such recommendations use the 'hold' nomenclature.

Womack (1996) examines data over the years 1989–91, and finds evidence that downgrades are accompanied by significantly negative abnormal returns. He only examines stock recommendation revisions to and from extremes. Three day returns centered on the date the stock recommendations are released are as follows. Added-to-buy results in a positive 3.3% return, whereas added-to-sell results in a negative 4.3% return. He also looks at abnormal volume, which is high on days before and after the change in stock recommendation. Additionally, he finds strong 'post-recommendation drift' for one month after buy changes, and up to six months after sell changes. Including the drift over the several months, he finds a positive 5% increase in prices after changes to buy, and –11% for changes to sell. Finally, he documents that the market reaction for recommendations on smaller firms is larger than for bigger firms.

Target prices

On 16 December 1998, Henry Blodget of CIBC Oppenheimer & Co. updated his 12-month target price on Amazon from US$150 to US$400, eclipsing other analysts' target prices. The shares of Amazon subsequently achieved the US$400 per share level, and Henry Blodget became a household name among internet analysts.

Target prices are analysts' forecasts of the stock price per share for some horizon. Most target price forecasts are stated in terms of a '12 month' horizon. However, there are also target prices specified as 'six month', '18 month', and other horizons. What these horizons mean is not exactly clear. For example, suppose that on 1 January 2002 an analyst states, 'We have a 12 month target price of US$50 on the common stock of XYZ Company.' Does this mean that the analyst is forecasting the price at the end of the 12 month period (1 January 2003) to be US$50 per share? Or does it mean that on at least one day between 1 January 2002 and 1 January 2003 the stock of XYZ will hit US$50 per share, but not necessarily maintain that level?

Bradshaw and Brown (2002) examined a large number of target prices issued by analysts during 1997–99. To compare target prices across a large number of firms, they scaled each target price by the actual stock price for the day prior to the date the analyst issued the target price. The distribution of 52,318 12 month target prices is shown in Exhibit 5.4.

Exhibit 5.4 shows that analysts' target prices are almost uniformly optimistic, with target prices exceeding the current trading price. For the years 1997–99, analysts increasingly raised their target prices relative to current prices from a predicted 24% appreciation in 1997 to a 31% predicted appreciation in 1999. Although such annual levels of price appreciation seem abnormally high, so were the actual levels of price increases observed during this period. The question is, how well did these target price forecasts perform?

To assess the accuracy of target prices, it is necessary to commit to a 'definition' of what it means for a target price to be met or achieved. As noted above, one alternative is to deem a target price forecast to have been met if the closing price per share at the end of the 12 month horizon is at or above the target price forecast level. An alternative, lower hurdle is to deem a target price to have been achieved if the stock price meets the target price at any time during the 12 month horizon. Exhibit 5.5 shows the frequency that target prices are met under each of these two definitions. In addition, Exhibit 5.5 presents a third metric, which is the fraction of trading days during the 12 month horizon for which the actual stock price closed at or above the forecasted target price.

Exhibit 5.4

Analyst target prices

	1997	1998	1999	All periods
N	11,233	21,179	19,906	52,318
Mean	1.24	1.28	1.31	1.29
Minimum	0.85	0.83	0.84	0.84
1%	0.97	0.94	0.94	0.95
25%	1.14	1.12	1.16	1.14
Median	1.21	1.22	1.26	1.24
75%	1.31	1.38	1.42	1.39
99%	1.92	2.06	2.11	2.11
Maximum	2.40	2.38	2.42	2.43

Source: Authors' own.

Exhibit 5.5

Frequency target prices met

	1997	1998	1999
% target prices met at the end of 12 months	34.7	26.4	26.8
% of days that target prices were met	27.9	18.3	21.6
% of target prices met on at least one day	67.2	51.5	56.1

Source: Authors' own.

The overall assessment of target prices thus depends on the definition of what it means for a target price to be 'met.' If it is insisted that target prices reflect what the shares should be trading at or above at the end of the holding period, then target prices do not appear to be very accurate. Only 26–35% of target prices are achieved under this definition. However, if we view target prices as being accurate so long as the price attains the level of the target price forecast on at least one day during the forecast horizon, then target prices appear to be more accurate, with 51–67% of target prices being achieved.

In subsequent analysis, Bradshaw and Brown (2002), here as before, document several additional characteristics of target prices, which square well with intuition. First, overall upward market movements clearly enhance the accuracy of outstanding target price forecasts as the general trend of the market carries along all stocks. The years they examined are definitely characterized by overall upward market movements. Second, target prices for companies with more volatile stock prices are more likely to be achieved under the less restrictive definition whereby a target price is accurate if the stock closes at or above the target price forecast level on at least one day. Third, the more optimistic the target price relative to the current stock price, the less likely it is that the target price forecast is achieved, regardless of how accuracy is defined.

A study by Brav and Lehavy (2002) examined the market reaction to announcements of target price forecasts. They found that, on average, abnormal returns during the five day window surrounding the release of target prices ranged from −3.9% for downward revisions to +3.2% for upward revisions. These magnitudes are on par with those surrounding earnings forecast revisions. However, the magnitudes of these stock price movements are well below the overall levels of forecasted price appreciation over current levels (for example, 29% on average, as noted above). Since most target prices have a horizon of one year, it is hard to imagine that the discrepancy between the market reactions to target price announcements and the returns implicit in the levels of forecasted target price appreciation is subject to routine discounting. The likely explanation is that the market is aware of the over optimistic nature of target price forecasts, and rationally discounts for this optimism.

The relation between long-term growth forecasts, recommendations, and target price forecasts

Even though target prices appear to be very optimistic, their importance cannot be understated. Analysts frequently justify their stock recommendations by the level of the target price relative to the current price. Moreover, target prices are strongly related to the analysts' long-term growth projections. Consider the following 15 January 1999 stock recommendation on Dialogic issued by an analyst from John Kinnard:

> We value Dialogic's shares based on one times its long-term growth rate of 15%. We are initiating coverage of DLGC with a BUY rating for aggressive growth investors and a US$32 price target based on 15 times our 2000 EPS estimate of US$2.14.

The day prior to the release of the report, DLGC stock closed trading at US$24.50. Thus, the analysts' target price was just over 22% above the current price. Within five days after the release of the report, the stock had climbed to US$30.00.

The recommendation not only justifies the purchase of the stock based on its target price of US$32 relative to the current trading price, but also provides an example of a frequent method of reporting target prices, the PEG ratio, which incorporates the earnings per share forecast and the long-term earnings growth (LTG) forecast. The combination of the P/E ratio and the LTG projection form a ratio referred to as the 'P/E-to-Growth' or 'PEG' ratio. Numerous financial sites exist which use PEG as a stock screen (for example, www.stockselector.com and www.fool.com/pegulator), and this metric is not new. Even Peter Lynch advocates the use of PEG: 'The P/E ratio of any company that's fairly priced will equal its growth rate. We use this measure all the time in analyzing stocks for the mutual funds' (Lynch, 1989).

Formally, PEG is defined as:

$$PEG = \frac{P/E}{LTG}$$

where P is the current stock price, E is the forecasted earnings per share, and LTG is the long-term earnings growth forecast stated in %. Thus, the PEG ratio is simply a ratio of the forward P/E ratio to the long-term earnings growth forecast. Advocates of this ratio claim that a 'normal' value of PEG that characterizes a fairly valued stock would be 1. General rules of thumb are that PEG ratios below 0.5 would be akin to strong buy recommendations, and those above 1.5 would indicate a strong sell.

Exhibit 5.6

Correlation between stock recommendations and target price estimates

Correlation between:	TP/P	TP_{PE1}/P	TP_{PE2}/P	TP_{PEG1}/P	TP_{PEG2}/P
Stock recommendation	0.33	−0.07	−0.04	0.39	0.38

Source: Authors' own.

Assuming that a fairly valued stock has a PEG of 1, the equation can be rearranged to solve for price:

$$P = E \times LTG$$

In the recommendation for Dialogic, the analyst has essentially used the PEG based valuation model, calculating the target price as:

$$Target\ price = 15 \times US\$2.14 = US\$32.10 \approx US\$32.00$$

Bradshaw (2002) collected a sample of analysts' recommendations, and measured the correlation between the levels of the stock recommendation (coded on a one to five scale, with higher numbers corresponding to more favorable recommendations) and several target prices and target price estimates. Exhibit 5.6 summarizes correlations between stock recommendations and the various target price estimates.

In Exhibit 5.6, all target price estimates are scaled by the current stock price per share (P). TP is the analysts' disclosed target price forecast. TP_{PE1} (TP_{PE2}) is a P/E multiple based estimate of target price using the median industry P/E multiples for one year (two year) ahead earnings forecasts. TP_{PEG1} (TP_{PEG2}) is a PEG based estimate of target price calculated using one year (two year) ahead earnings forecasts.

What is clear from the correlations is the strong correspondence between PEG based target prices and the analysts' actual target prices (TP/P). However, target price estimates based on industry P/E multiples are not correlated with analysts' stock recommendations at all. The correlations of −0.07 between stock recommendation levels and TP_{PE1}/P and of −0.04 between stock recommendations levels and TP_{PE2}/P are both statistically equal to zero. In contrast, the correlations between both PEG based target price estimates are larger in magnitude than the correlation between the analysts' disclosed target prices.

Analysts seem to rely heavily on their forecasts of accounting earnings and of long-term earnings growth in establishing target prices that support stock recommendations, even though their forecasts of long-term earnings growth are extremely over optimistic, as noted above. Furthermore, these forecasts are impounded into valuations (target prices) through a relatively unsophisticated heuristic rather than through a rigorous valuation model, as one might have assumed.

Summary

Whether this means that investors should be wary of long-term growth forecasts, recommendations, or target prices is an open question. Clearly, at least some investors respond to the release of such information by analysts. Does the market reaction reflect unsophisticated investors relying too heavily on these items? Is the market reaction a result of sophisticated traders taking positions knowing the predictable consequences of analysts revising such forecasts and recommendations? These questions are currently unanswered, but provide a fruitful area for future research.

References

Long-term earnings growth forecasts:

Dechow, P.M., and R.G. Sloan (1997), 'Returns to Contrarian Investment Strategies: Tests of Naive Expectations Hypotheses', *Journal of Financial Economics,* Vol. 43, pp. 3–27.

La Porta, R. (1996), 'Expectations and the Cross-Section of Stock Returns', *The Journal of Finance*, December, pp. 1715–1742.

Stock recommendations:

McNichols, M., and P. O'Brien (1977), 'Self Selection and Analyst Coverage', *Journal of Accounting Research*, Vol. 35, pp. 167–199.

Womack, K.L. (1996), 'Do Brokerage Analysts' Recommendations Have Investment Value?', *The Journal of Finance,* Vol. 51, March, pp. 137–167.

Target prices:

Bradshaw, M.T. (2002), 'The Use of Target Prices to Justify Sell-Side Analysts' Stock Recommendations', *Accounting Horizons*, March, pp. 27–41.

Bradshaw, M.T., and L.D. Brown (2002), 'An Examination of Sell-Side Analysts' Abilities to Predict Target Prices', Working Paper, Harvard University and Georgia State University, June.

Brav, A., and R. Lehavy (2001), 'An Empirical Analysis of Analysts' Target Prices: Short Term Informativeness and Long Term Dynamics', Working Paper, Duke University and University of California at Berkeley, May.

Studies looking at the relation among these outputs:

Bradshaw, M.T. (2002), 'How Do Analysts Use Their Earnings Forecasts in Generating Stock Recommendations?', Working Paper, Harvard Business School.

Lynch, P. (1989), *One Up on Wall Street*, Simon and Schuster, New York, p. 198.

Chapter 6

Non-GAAP measures of earnings

'Pro Forma Normalized Recurring Earnings Before Interest, Taxes, Depreciation, and Amortization' (PFNREBITDA).

Earnings number reported by Quest Communications International

For years, investors have focused their attention on earnings calculated in accordance with generally accepted accounting principles (GAAP) established by the regulatory organizations and their predecessors. However, recently companies have been reporting an ever-widening array of alternatively calculated earnings figures. Wall Street has embraced these definitions of earnings, although these are not explicitly defined or sanctioned by any of the regulatory overseers. These definitions are known by such names as 'pro forma', 'normalized', 'cash earnings', and a host of other such names.

In this chapter, this trend is examined, and we provide two sides of the argument for and against the use of pro forma accounting numbers. Should investors pay attention to these numbers, or should they view them as an attempt by managers to hoodwink them into believing earnings are rosier than they are?

Anecdotal evidence

An exhaustive report on the subject by Keon (2001) looked at the differences between GAAP earnings and pro forma earnings. Reported earnings 'could be whatever the company could convince analysts were correct', said Keon, a former executive at I/B/E/S. He speculates that when the gaps began they were driven by two changes in corporate practices: the merger and acquisition boom, and the re-structuring movement. Many companies, due to a need to show the results from an acquisition or to deal with poor performance, discontinued, sold or cut back on marginal operations, thereby taking a one time charge against earnings. By the 1990s, companies like General Motors were taking charges due to pension liabilities. Since this was no change in the actual liability, companies excluded these charges from earnings. By the late 1990s, internet firms had taken this practice to extremes, excluding marketing costs, shipping costs, and other normal expenses associated with doing business.

This has caused investors to push analysts to take a deeper look at pro forma earnings. Merrill Lynch in early 2002 told its analysts to use a variety of methods to judge financial performance, rather than relying on pro forma earnings, when reporting on a company. In an internal memo, Merrill said it was adopting in its research 'the use of broad measures beyond pro forma earnings to evaluate a company's quality of earnings with the objective of establishing an enhanced standard of accountability and transparency for our clients'. The goal is to use the tougher GAAP standards more rigorously in evaluating firms.

Academic evidence

Although not permitted in Securities and Exchange Commission (SEC) filings, pro forma and similarly defined definitions of earnings frequently appear in corporate news releases. Moreover, the financial press has been part of the acceptance of such numbers by routinely disseminating them without much further thought until the practice was widespread.

The formal evidence on pro forma earnings is recent, reflecting how recent the phenomenon is. In this section, a number of questions that have been investigated recently are reviewed. The first question is why pro forma earnings have become so important. Many outspoken market observers attribute the popularity of pro forma earnings to a decline in corporate managers' ethical standards. However, other observers, including SEC officials, argue that managers are simply trying to filter out 'noise' in accounting numbers that is a side effect of bad accounting rules. Additionally, some suggest that overall structural shifts in the corporate reporting environment provide an explanation.

A second issue examined focuses attention on the pros and cons of the growing popularity of pro forma earnings. On the pro side, pro forma earnings can allow management to provide investors with a better indication of recurring earnings and hence long run cash flow. On the con side, however, management also may exclude recurring expenses from pro forma earnings, which may lead to inflated investor expectations. Some researchers have concluded that the objectives of pro forma earnings need to be more clearly defined, and that rules for the consistent preparation and presentation of pro forma earnings need to be established and enforced.

Documentation of the phenomenon

There is no standard set of rules or principles to guide the preparation of pro forma earnings. Thus, pro forma earnings are like a pasta primavera (everyone has their own special recipe).

The initial research in this area uses the actual reported earnings number promulgated by the analyst tracking services (I/B/E/S, First Call and Zacks) as the proxy for pro forma earnings, and that is what we discuss first. These services sometimes disagree among themselves as to the appropriate number for reported earnings. The earnings number reported by I/B/E/S has the most complete historical database.

Through the early 1990s, differences between pro forma earnings and GAAP earnings generally were restricted to special or non-recurring items such as asset impairments, restructuring charges, and other non-operating items. I/B/E/S's glossary explaining its terms and conventions acknowledges the exclusion of such items, and explains that the tracking service

> receives an analyst's forecast after discontinued operations, extraordinary charges, and other non-operating items have been backed out. While this is far and away the best method for valuing a company, it often causes a discrepancy when a company reports earnings. I/B/E/S adjusts reported earnings to match analysts' forecasts on both an annual and quarterly basis. This is why I/B/E/S actuals may not agree with other published actuals (Compustat).

As the recent earnings reporting trend took hold, companies started to exclude more items from pro forma earnings. The vast majority are expenses and losses, so their exclusion has the effect of increasing pro forma earnings relative to GAAP earnings. The exclusion of

Exhibit 6.1

Wall Street versus GAAP earnings per share (scaled by price), 1985–99

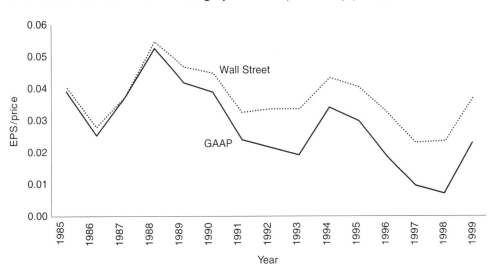

Source: Bradshaw and Sloan (2001).

these items often is justified on the basis that they are non-cash charges. Examples include amortization and depreciation charges, stock compensation expenses, deferred tax charges, and losses at affiliated and subsidiary companies. However, only a subset of accruals is reversed, so the resulting pro forma earnings number does not correspond to the cash from operations reported in the cash flow statement. Some additional cash items also are excluded on the basis that they are not relevant to evaluating the firm's performance. Examples include costs related to mergers and acquisitions, research and development, interest, and taxes. Due to the non-standardized nature of such reporting, investors are subject to a dizzying array of earnings numbers.

Exhibit 6.1 illustrates the growing gap between pro forma and GAAP earnings. It presents annual pro forma and GAAP earnings yields (annual earnings per share scaled by stock price) averaged across all U.S. equities covered by I/B/E/S for the years 1985–99. GAAP are defined as earnings before extraordinary and discontinued operations, so that these GAAP defined non-recurring items do not contribute to the results. Exhibit 6.1 also includes firms for which pro forma earnings and GAAP earnings are the same, which has the effect of understating the average differences for firms with differences between pro forma and GAAP earnings.

Exhibit 6.1 shows a large and growing disparity between pro forma and GAAP earnings since the late 1980s. The items excluded from pro forma earnings are almost universally expenses and losses, so pro forma earnings exhibit a substantial upward bias relative to GAAP earnings. In recent years, the disparity has been so great that average earnings yields using pro forma earnings have been about 3%, double the 1.5% rise in average earnings yields using GAAP earnings.

A more detailed examination of the data emphasized two key factors in the growing difference between the two numbers. First is the increase in the proportion of firms for which pro forma earnings differ from GAAP earnings. Second is the steady expansion of the list of items that are excluded from pro forma earnings.

The analyst tracking services and the sell side analysts whose earnings forecasts they track represent financial intermediaries who do not work for the companies reporting earnings. The evidence discussed thus far indicates that securities analysts and the tracking services are responsible for the production of pro forma earnings. Companies reporting earnings are still required to comply with GAAP in their formal financial statement filings with investors and the SEC. However, research shows systematic evidence that corporate managers promulgate the use of pro forma earnings by defining and emphasizing the particular earnings definition that they would like the analysts and analyst tracking services to adopt.

Corporate managers use press releases containing their quarterly earnings announcements to inform analysts of the definition of pro forma earnings they wish to promulgate. A recent study presents the results of reading through a large sample of press releases. The analysis was restricted to earnings announcements in which the pro forma earnings number reported by I/B/E/S differed from the GAAP earnings number reported by *Compustat*.

Dividing a sample into two sub-samples, each consisting of 200 quarterly earnings announcements, researchers randomly obtained earnings announcements. The first was selected randomly from earnings announcements in 1986–87, during which there were few differences between GAAP and pro forma earnings. The second sub-sample was selected randomly from earnings announcements in 1998–99, by which time the disparity between pro forma and GAAP earnings had become substantial.

If corporate managers have taken a proactive role in promulgating pro forma earnings, then there will be a substantial increase across these two sub-samples both in the proportion of press releases that define and report a distinct pro forma earnings number, and in the relative emphasis placed on that number. Thus, indicator variables are tracked that identify whether management reported a pro forma earnings number, a GAAP earnings number, or both. Further, if management reported both pro forma and GAAP earnings numbers, the order in which the two numbers were presented is noted.

Exhibit 6.2 summarizes these findings and highlights corporate management's role in promulgating pro forma earnings.

More than 80% of the earnings announcements in the 1986–87 period reported only GAAP earnings, but this figure dropped to less than 30% by 1998–99. Moreover, the fre-

Exhibit 6.2

Order of earnings per share presentation

Period	GAAP only	GAAP then pro forma	Pro forma then GAAP	Pro forma only	All
1986–87	165	22	13	0	200
	(82.5%)	(11.0%)	(6.5%)	(0.0%)	(100%)
1998–99	57	56	84	3	200
	(28.5%)	(28.0%)	(42.0%)	(1.5%)	(100%)
Total	222	78	97	3	400

Source: Authors' own.

Exhibit 6.3

Price sensitivity of Wall Street and GAAP earnings, 1986–97

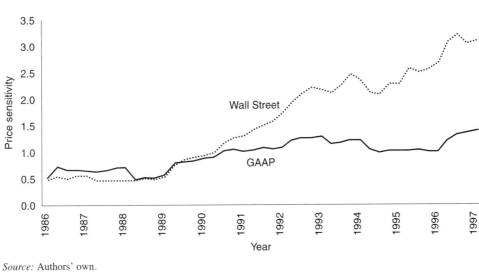

Source: Authors' own.

quency with which pro forma earnings represented the first number reported in the earnings announcement rose from just 6.5% in 1986–87 to 42% in 1998–99.

Additionally, Exhibit 6.2 shows a growing tendency for GAAP earnings to be relegated toward the end of the earnings announcement. During the 1998–99 period, the pro forma earnings number typically appeared in the first or second paragraph, whereas the GAAP earnings number on average was delayed until the fourth paragraph.

The previous evidence highlights the popularity of pro forma earnings among managers and analysts, but is silent on the question of whether investors use pro forma earnings.

Researchers have also looked at the relationship between the two competing definitions of earnings and contemporaneous stock prices. First, they examine the sensitivity of stock returns to earnings. Sensitivity measures the magnitude of the stock price response to earnings surprises. A higher sensitivity indicates that investors view the reported earnings measure as more indicative of long run recurring trends in firm performance. Second, they examine the ability of earnings surprises to explain stock returns. Higher explanatory power can be attributable both to providing better information about long run recurring firm performance and to providing better information about short run innovations in firm performance.

Exhibit 6.3 plots trends in the average sensitivity of stock prices to both pro forma and GAAP earnings over the last two decades.

Through the early 1990s, when there was little divergence between pro forma earnings and GAAP earnings, the sensitivities were similar. However, during the 1990s, when pro forma earnings diverged significantly from GAAP earnings, there was dramatic improvement in the sensitivity of stock prices to pro forma earnings relative to GAAP earnings. Investors clearly interpret pro forma earnings to be a better indicator of long run recurring firm performance.

Exhibit 6.4 plots the explanatory power of pro forma earnings versus GAAP earnings over the past two decades.

Exhibit 6.4

Ability of Wall Street and GAAP earnings to explain stock prices, 1986–97

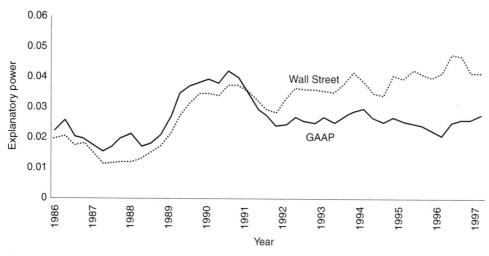

Source: Authors' own.

Again, Exhibit 6.4 indicates that the ability of pro forma and GAAP earnings to explain variation in stock prices was similar until the early 1990s, while afterward there was a clear shift in favor of pro forma earnings. This evidence indicates that investors view pro forma earnings as more relevant than GAAP earnings, and that the increased relevance arises from investors' perception that pro forma earnings provide a better indication of long run recurring firm performance.

At first glance, it may appear that the stock price results provide a ringing endorsement of pro forma earnings. Despite the ad hoc and unregulated manner in which pro forma earnings are produced, they seem to be of greater relevance to investors than GAAP earnings.

However, this presumes that investors correctly interpret the implications of pro forma earnings for firm value. An alternative theory is that investors are getting hoodwinked into relying too heavily on pro forma earnings. After all, these are the earnings numbers that managers highlight, and analyst tracking services and the business press use, as they disseminate information on earnings surprises. It is possible that investors simply don't dig deeply enough into the earnings announcements and SEC filings to figure out the differences between pro forma earnings and GAAP earnings.

The latter interpretation is worrisome, since pro forma earnings ignore so many expenses and losses. These expenses and losses usually represent very real operating costs that are associated with past, present or future cash outflow. If investors naively are pricing companies based on inflated pro forma earnings numbers, significant overvaluation may result. Such overvaluation will not correct itself until investors realize that pro forma earnings do not coincide with the long run cash generating ability of the firm. GAAP earnings generally preserve the long run correspondence between earnings and cash flow, and so are less susceptible to this problem.

Conjectures on the cause of the phenomenon

Overall, research findings suggest that the rise of pro forma earnings is attributable to corporate management, security analysts, and the analyst tracking services. Regulators and business journalists have suggested that the rise of pro forma earnings is indicative of a growing lack of good faith on the part of these parties. However, two concurrent structural shifts in the financial reporting environment have helped legitimize the rise of the pro forma earnings phenomenon.

The first is dramatic advances in information technology that have made it possible for earnings announcements to be widely disseminated to investors long before the formal dissemination of the required SEC filings. These earnings announcements and the conference calls that often accompany them now are the most important financial reporting events for many large companies.

However, these events take place largely outside of regulations pertaining to the preparation of the financial statements, so managers have considerable latitude with respect to the information reported. In this essentially unregulated environment, it is inevitable that a small number of aggressive managers push the envelope in trying to put their firm's performance in the best possible light. Other firms then feel pressure to follow suit in order to remain competitive in the capital markets. For these reasons, the outdated SEC-mandated financial reporting framework may need updating to encompass the fair and consistent reporting of earnings announcements.

The second key shift in the financial reporting environment is the Financial Accounting Standards Board's move away from an income statement approach and toward a balance sheet approach in setting GAAP. The increased emphasis on the balance sheet can be traced to the introduction of SFAC No. 6 in 1985, and is clearly evident in subsequent accounting standards such as SFAS No. 109, SFAS No. 121, SFAS No. 142, and SFAS No. 144. The balance sheet approach shifts attention from trying to match costs to revenues on the income statement toward trying to appropriately value assets and liabilities on the balance sheet. However, the realization principle is retained, so the balance sheet still fails to capture the most important asset from an investor perspective (cash flow associated with anticipated future sales).

The essence of this shift is that, instead of amortizing many assets to the income statement in a systematic manner, firms are encouraged to take occasional impairments to assets or adjustments to valuation allowances. The result is that income statements are now routinely peppered with non-recurring special charges associated with these balance sheet adjustments.

Exhibits 6.5 and 6.6 illustrate the increasing importance of special items. Exhibit 6.5 reports trends in the proportion of firms reporting negative special items. Exhibit 6.6 reports trends in the magnitude of special items as a proportion of total expenses.

Exhibit 6.5 shows that the frequency of negative special items has more than doubled from less than 10% to more than 20%, while Exhibit 6.6 shows that they have increased in magnitude from less than 1% to more than 2% of corporate expenses.

Investors who are interested in the long run recurring performance of a company clearly wish to back out these non-recurring special items. The evolution of pro forma earnings represents an attempt by managers and security analysts to assist in that task. However, this process can be gamed by unscrupulous managers. In what is described as the 'big bath phenomenon', large pools of recurring costs occasionally are charged to the income statement under the guise of a non-recurring balance sheet adjustment. With these costs out of the picture, the company can report a larger pro forma earnings number on an ongoing basis.

Exhibit 6.5

Percentage of companies recording write-offs, 1985–97

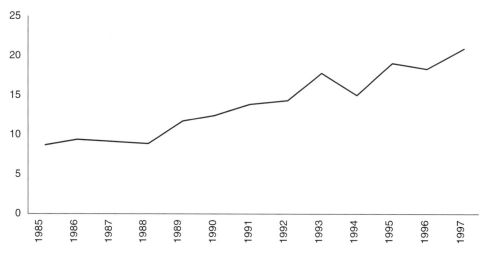

Source: Authors' own.

Exhibit 6.6

Average write-off as a percentage of total operating expenses, 1985–97

Source: Authors' own.

Discussion of the pros and cons

The key advantage of pro forma earnings is that they focus on the recurring components of firm performance. Investors typically value companies by discounting the expected future cash flow. To the extent that pro forma earnings are purged of the non-recurring special charges that now pervade GAAP earnings, they provide investors with a key valuation input.

However, it is important to remember one key advantage of GAAP earnings. They typically satisfy clean surplus, meaning that, over the long run, GAAP earnings and cash flow are equal. In other words, timing represents the only difference between GAAP earnings and cash flow. This property of GAAP earnings provides a clear theoretical link between earnings and firm value, and an important practical limitation on the extent to which GAAP earnings can deviate from the underlying cash flow. This property is lost with the move to pro forma earnings. The systematic exclusion of expenses and losses means that in the long run pro forma earnings exceed cash flow. The extent to which long run pro forma earnings exceed long run future cash flow is limited only by managers' ingenuity in taking big baths and excluding other costs from pro forma earnings.

Investors demand an earnings number that provides a good basis for forecasting recurring future cash flow. The proliferation of special items in GAAP earnings has made it an increasingly irrelevant indicator of future cash flow.

Summary

Pro forma earnings represent an attempt to restore some of this relevance. However, the wide latitude open to management and analysts in defining pro forma earnings can result in an unreliable number that most likely significantly overstates recurring future cash flow.

The timely dissemination of a relevant and reliable measure of periodic operating performance is crucial to the efficient operation of capital markets. To this end, it is necessary that the SEC and the accounting profession work with management and analysts to provide a more reliable and unbiased alternative to the current pro forma earnings situation.

References

Bradshaw, M.T., and R.G. Sloan (2001), 'Pro Forma Earnings Fill a Reporting Vacuum', *Investor Relations Quarterly*, Vol. 4, No. 4.

Bradshaw, M.T., and R.G. Sloan (2002), 'GAAP versus The Street: An Empirical Assessment of Two Alternative Definitions of Earnings', *Journal of Accounting Research*, March, Vol. 40, No. 1, pp. 41–66.

Keon, Ed (2001), *What's the P/E Ratio of the S&P 500?*, Prudential Equity Research, 29 October.

Chapter 7

Earnings management

The only real gauge we have of success is profit.

Rex Beach

Do managers manipulate earnings? Almost anyone familiar with the financial reporting process would not hesitate to answer the question. Most people would respond, 'Yes, of course managers manage earnings.' However, what does it mean to 'manage' earnings? Most observers would agree that any deliberate intervention in the accounting process aimed at affecting reported financial numbers would fall under the definition of earnings management. However, there seems to be no accepted definition of earnings management.

Nevertheless, there seems to be a general consensus among academics, regulators, and the investment community that earnings manipulation is characterized by managerial intent to paint a picture of firm performance that is not accurate. Additionally, most believe that earnings management is widespread. However, is there hard evidence to support this claim? Why would managers care so much about managing earnings? How can we measure whether earnings have been managed? What has been documented regarding the pervasiveness of earnings management? In this chapter, there is a very brief description of how researchers have viewed earnings management, and we summarize a small but representative sampling of the evidence.

What is earnings management?

There is a continuum of what might be defined as earnings management. At one extreme is outright fraud – recording fictitious sales or assets, for example. This is beyond the scope of earnings management, and is not what we typically think of as earnings management. On the other extreme are operating decisions. For example, managers might decide to delay certain research and development activities until a future reporting period in order to keep from depressing current reported earnings, but no accounting policies are violated. While we can view this as earnings management, again, this is typically not what we think of when we speak of earnings management.

In between these extremes are a number of forms of activities that are typically considered to be classical earnings management, including the structuring of transactions to achieve a desired accounting treatment, income smoothing, classificatory earnings management, and others.

In colloquial terms, most of us consider earnings management as occurring when, all else equal, managers exercise judgment that results in higher earnings. As a specific example, consider the rules governing the accounting for stock option compensation. The rules under the 'intrinsic value method' (which everyone follows, as opposed to the 'fair value method') specify that any excess over stock price on the date of grant to the employee over the option's exercise price be expensed as part of employee compensation. As a consequence of this rule, pretty much every stock option granted carries an exercise price equal to the stock price on the date of grant. *Voilà*! Under the intrinsic value method, the compensation expense is then calculated as:

$$\text{Compensation expense} = \text{Stock price} - \text{Exercise price} = 0$$

Consequently, if we allow the definition of earnings manipulation to extend to such decisions as what strike price managers recommend to the compensation committee, then it would seem that all managers are manipulating earnings, since managers (with the assistance of the compensation committee of their board of directors) almost always ensure that exercise prices equal stock prices on the date of grant.

To further appreciate why it is so difficult to pinpoint a definition of earnings management, note that accrual accounting by nature actually aims to reduce fluctuations in earnings that would otherwise be reported under alternative measurement principles, for example, cash accounting. The provision of regular charges for depreciation expense 'smoothes' earnings by allocating large capital expenditures over numerous periods, rather than by recording the expenditure in a single period. Accounting standard setters have concluded that matching the cost of a capital expenditure over the periods that it provides benefits provides a closer description of economic reality. The bottom line is that this accounting procedure acts to smooth earnings, but few would classify depreciation as 'earnings management' or 'earnings manipulation.'

Finally, there are a number of ways in which managers can affect reported numbers in financial statements. Managers select among several acceptable accounting method alternatives (for example, straight-line versus accelerated depreciation methods), often must make estimates for a particular accounting method choice (for example, depreciable life, estimated salvage value, and the like), and can make 'real' operating decisions that directly affect the financial statements (for example, to delay replacing an old piece of equipment). Collectively, any of these decisions may impact reported earnings. Thus, when thinking about earnings management, it is important to be clear as to exactly the kind of earnings management in which one is interested.

Exhibit 7.1 is taken from a paper by Patricia Dechow and Doug Skinner of the University of Michigan Business School. Exhibit 7.1 reflects examples across a continuum of earnings management, from operating decisions (not in violation of GAAP) to fraud (violations of GAAP). In between are examples of discretion available to managers within GAAP. It is the central section that we are concerned with in this chapter.

Although the definition of earnings management is subject to interpretation, we proceed with the understanding that we are primarily interested in 'classical' earnings management. The easiest way to limit the definition of what we mean by classical is to specifically exclude certain activities. In this chapter, earnings management excludes (i) fraud, (ii) accounting method choices, and (iii) actual operating decisions, including those directly affecting operations as well as those in which a manager strategically structures a transaction to achieve a certain desired accounting treatment. Having said this, it is important to note that it is generally impossible to isolate classical earnings management from any of these other types of earnings management, and any time we conclude a manager is 'managing earnings,' we do so with the caveat that there may be other less incriminating decisions being made that relate to operations, rather than an attempt to manage earnings.

Exhibit 7.1

What is a violation of GAAP?

Within GAAP		Violation of GAAP
Operating decisions	*Accounting decisions*	*Fraud*
Accelerating or delaying expenditures on research and development	Aggressive or conservative recognition of provisions or reserves (eg, bad debt allowance, estimated liabilities, etc.)	Recording fictitious sales
Setting stock option exercise prices equal to the actual stock price on the date of grant	Big bath write-offs that record expenses in the current period that would have been recorded in prior of future periods	Increasing ending inventory balances (to reduce cost of goods sold) by falsifying inventory records
Structuring leases to attain operating lease accounting treatment	Subjective decisions regarding 'technological feasibility' in deciding if and when software development costs should be capitalized	Establishment of reserves for possible future events

Source: Dechow and Skinner (2000).

Why would a manager manipulate earnings?

Given the high level of attention given to detecting earnings management, there must be reasons to suspect that managers care about reported earnings enough to manipulate them. One reason managers might manipulate earnings is 'because everybody else does'. If all managers artificially increase or smooth their firms' earnings, then a manager who does not do so might be doing themselves and their shareholders a disservice.

Generally, we can classify most incentives to manipulate earnings into two categories: (1) to influence stock prices or (2) to affect the parameters of various contracts that incorporate accounting-based covenants.

Managers have clear incentives to care about stock prices. First, the increase in the use of stock-based compensation over time has intensified managers' focus on their stock prices. Under a typical stock option plan, managers' compensation is linearly related to stock prices. For example, for every US$1.00 per share increase in stock price, the manager can realize additional income of US$1.00 times the number of stock options they have available for exercise. In addition to pure compensation reasons, managers care about stock prices to the extent that there is a market for corporate control whereby outside parties can purchase a firm whose stock price has sufficiently declined, and then replace the current management with their own managers. Relatedly, managers' career concerns are heavily reliant on their perceived ability to increase shareholder value. Thus, there is a clear link between managers' incentives to manipulate earnings and stock prices.

Second, managers aware of the use of accounting numbers in various contracts have incentives to affect the reported numbers. In addition to compensation by means of stock options whose value is dependent on stock prices, managers are also compensated under bonus plans. Frequently, bonus plans specify payments contingent on various accounting measures, such as net income, return on equity, sales growth, and the like. Similar to the incentives tied to stock options, managers are frequently aware of how reported numbers impact their bonuses. Additionally, firms frequently are subject to contracts with outside entities, where the terms of the contracts specify accounting number or ratio requirements. The most common form of these are debt covenants, which customarily specify a number of accounting ratios that must be maintained for the firm to be in compliance with the debt agreement.

Is earnings management bad?

There are two views investors may take on the desirability of earnings management. On one hand, earnings management reduces the integrity of financial information; hence the practice is undesirable from an investor's perspective. This seems to be the most common perspective, often the basis for conclusions that managers use 'accounting tricks' aimed at fooling investors. On the other hand, another perspective is that current investors desire earnings management in order to maintain or elevate prices at which they may sell their shares to the next generation of shareholders. The latter perspective seems to be related to the expectation game played on Wall Street in recent years, where investors ironically expect to be surprised with a management announcement that earnings are one penny above what had been expected by analysts. The recent past is full of stock prices declines when managers announce earnings just meet expectations.

Whether you view earnings management as good or bad depends on whether you are a potential buyer or seller. Of course, all else equal, it should be preferred that managers report an unbiased account of their performance. However, if one manager uses discretion available in accounting rules to artificially enhance their performance, then other managers are more likely to also engage in such behavior. The presumed result is a cascading of pervasive earnings management, which is the subject of much media coverage.

Detecting and measuring earnings management

To detect earnings management, we need to have some benchmark of what earnings would have been absent any manipulation by the manager. With such a benchmark, identification of the amount of earnings management is easy. It is simply the difference between the benchmark and what was actually reported. However, it is impossible to know what earnings would have been. That is the million-dollar question. To cope with the benchmarking problem, one must somehow estimate what earnings would have been. Clearly, this is a difficult task, riddled with measurement error. It is for this reason that academics have had such difficulty documenting earnings management. There is no simple algorithm for detecting earnings management. However, given the strong correlation between earnings and stock prices, investors should be aware of what is known about managers' tendencies to manipulate earnings.

The simplest benchmark of what earnings would have been absent manipulation, say for a particular quarter, is to assume that earnings would have been the same as those reported in the corresponding quarter from last year. So, if last year's earnings were US\$X per share and this year's reported earnings were US\$Y per share, then the amount of earnings management is calculated as Y–X. Early analysis of earnings usually began with this assumption, which specifies that earnings follow a random walk. This is a not very appealing, however, because the underlying assumption implicit in a random walk is that 'real' earnings are not expected to change from their most recent realization. In other words, earnings are not expected to grow, but rather are random, which is clearly not intuitive or descriptive of historic earnings.

A slight enhancement is to assume some sort of expected trend in earnings. For example, if we assumed that, barring manager intervention, real earnings would grow at a rate of $r\%$ each year, then expected earnings this year would be $(1 + r)*X$, and earnings management would be calculated as $Y-[(1 +r)*X]$. Here, the implicit assumption is that real earnings trend smoothly. If earnings actually jump around due to unexpected events such as competitor moves, economic cycles, or changing customer preferences, then we should reasonably expect an erratic pattern of real earnings.

Were we to attempt to quantify earnings management by the above method, we could actually be measuring things backwards. Managers with a smooth trend in reported earnings would be deemed to be least likely to be manipulation earnings. However, in fact, managers who report a smoothly trending earnings pattern might be those who are managing earnings most actively. Indeed, one of the ways researchers have identified firms that are potentially managing earnings is to measure how closely reported earnings follow a trend. This is done by calculating firm-specific variances of reported earnings relative to a hypothetical smoothly trending earnings pattern. Firms with lowest variances of reported earnings (smoothest) are hypothesized to be those who are managing earnings the most.

Another way to measure earnings management is to forgo trying to measure 'unmanaged' earnings and instead use analysts' earnings forecasts as the expectation of earnings. Managers who manage earnings to achieve the forecasts or slightly exceed them are then candidates for possible earnings management. However, a problem with this method is that managers are a primary source of information for analysts devising forecasts. Therefore, managers may be able to manage the analysts' forecasts rather than managing earnings *per se*.

Nondiscretionary and discretionary accounting accruals

Due to the problems with the above, those interested in assessing earnings management use multiple methods, and rely on the 'weight' of the evidence. To date, the most widely used method is the assessment of managers' use of accounting accruals to manipulate earnings.

Accounting accruals are the non-cash transactions recorded in the financial statements that are aimed at providing a more complete picture of the results of operations than would a simple tracking of cash flows. The provision for depreciation of assets is typically the largest accrual for a company. As another example, products shipped to customers who have yet to pay as of the end of a reporting period are reflected via another accounting accrual ('Accounts Receivable') and record the related revenue in the current period. Similarly, at the end of a reporting period, employees will be entitled to receive pay for services provided to the firm, but are paid with a delay. To reflect the fact that employees are owed wages by the firm, managers record an expense in the current period and create an accounting accrual (for example, a liability called 'Wages Payable'). The previous chapter provided an in depth discussion of accounting accruals and an emphasis on how accruals can be used as a basis for determining 'earnings quality.'

Accruals can be income increasing or income decreasing. Generally, increases in working capital assets are income increasing accruals, because double entry bookkeeping implies that the increase in assets are typically accompanied by increases in a revenue (or decreases in expenses). An increase in accounts receivable is an example of an income increasing accrual. On the contrary, the opposite is true for decreases in working capital assets. An increase in the allowance for uncollectible accounts receivable decreases working capital assets (by offsetting gross accounts receivable), resulting in a decrease in income.

Similarly, increases in liabilities or other reserves are generally income-decreasing accruals, because such increases are typically associated with increases in expenses, which decrease income. For example, an increase in wages payable is accompanied by the recording of wages expense, which decreases income. Decreases in working capital assets generally reflect income-increasing accruals, though the logic can be a little confusing. All else equal, if a working capital liability declines, then you loosely can interpret this as reflecting expenses that managers did not have to record. To understand this, recall that accruals simply reconcile cash flows and accounting earnings. If wages payable decreases, for instance, then the firm must have paid more wages than were expensed.

The discretion available to managers relates directly to the amount and timing of accounting accruals, many of which are estimates. Thus, a common way to gauge whether there has been earnings management is to try and determine how much discretion managers have injected into the reported earnings figure. However, discretion is not necessarily bad. Managers can use discretion to make financial reports more informative. However, they can also use discretion strategically, and that is the focus of earnings management analysis.

How do you determine whether earnings contain 'too much' discretion? A common methodology that has been refined by a number of academics is to take total accruals, and split them into 'nondiscretionary' and 'discretionary' components. The discretionary component equates to the amount by which a manager has manipulated earnings up or down; the nondiscretionary component is supposed to reflect accruals warranted by the firm's economic performance. This methodology was initially applied by Jennifer Jones of the University of Chicago, who examined whether firms manage their earnings downward in response to import relief investigations by the U.S. International Trade Commission (Jones, 1991). Studies prior to hers had assumed that any changes in accruals between two reporting periods reflected discretionary accruals, an assumption tantamount to total accruals being completely nondiscretionary in the prior period.

Her model linked accruals to two financial statement items that should control for the underlying economics of the firm: changes in revenues (ΔRevenue = Revenue$_t$ – Revenue$_{t-1}$), and total property, plant, and equipment (PP&E).

$$\text{Total accruals} = B_0 + B_1 * \Delta \text{Revenue} + B_2 * \text{PP\&E}$$

Changes in revenues reflect growth in the top-line, which is expected to be accompanied by growth in nondiscretionary accruals, such as changes in accounts receivable, inventory, and accounts payable. Thus, the predicted sign of B_1 is positive. PP&E reflects the firm's investment in depreciable assets, which result in depreciation expense, a nondiscretionary accrual. The predicted sign of B_2 is negative, because depreciation is a negative accrual (income decreasing).

The above model is estimated using ordinary least squares regression. To provide a better specified regression model, all terms are typically divided by an appropriate scaling factor, such as lagged total assets. For simplicity, we assume that all variables are appropriately scaled. The estimates of the coefficients B_0, B_1, and B_2 (labeled b_0, b_1, and b_2) are used to estimate nondiscretionary accruals:

$$\text{Nondiscretionary accruals} = b_0 + b_1 * \Delta \text{Revenue} + b_2 * \text{PP\&E}$$

Exhibit 7.2

Estimation example

	Coefficient estimates from estimation period:		
	b_0	b_1	b_2
	4.50	0.20	−0.02

Parameter values from test period:	
ΔRevenue	PP&E
10	500

Source: Authors' own.

Discretionary accruals are estimated as the difference between total accruals and the estimate of nondiscretionary accruals:

$$\text{Discretionary accruals} = \text{Total accruals} - (b_0 + b_1 * \Delta\text{Revenue} + b_2 * \text{PP\&E})$$

A simplified example should clarify the estimation (see Exhibit 7.2).

Given the coefficient estimates and the values of the parameters from the test period, we would estimate nondiscretionary accruals as $4.50 + (0.20*10) - (0.02*500) = -3.50$. Suppose total accruals equaled 5. Then, discretionary accruals would be the difference between total accruals and estimated nondiscretionary accruals: $5 - (-3.50) = 8.50$. In this case, discretionary accruals would be income increasing, because their sign is positive.

Subsequent to the work by Jennifer Jones, researchers have made a number of refinements to the 'Jones model'. One refinement has been to change the specification of the estimate of nondiscretionary accruals. In the equation above, nondiscretionary accruals are estimated based partly on the change in revenue across two periods. This assumes that managers do not exercise any discretion over revenues as part of any earnings management. However, the majority of Accounting and Auditing Enforcement Releases issued by the Securities and Exchange Commission (SEC) relate to manipulations of revenues, so this assumption is likely to result in inferior estimates of nondiscretionary accruals when managers are actually manipulating revenues. Since revenues consist of both cash and non-cash (receivables) components, one modification to the Jones model is to maintain the estimation of the coefficients as above, but to estimate nondiscretionary accruals as:

$$\text{Nondiscretionary accruals} = b_0 + b_1 * (\Delta\text{Revenue} - \Delta\text{Accounts receivable}) + b_2 * \text{PP\&E}$$

The presumption in the modified Jones model is that all changes in credit (versus cash) revenues are due to manipulation of revenues by the manager. This is simply a different assumption than the one embedded in the original Jones model that revenues are not subject to managerial manipulation.

Additional explanatory variables may be added to (or replace) the right-hand side of the estimation of coefficients that determine nondiscretionary accruals. Studies focusing on a single industry, such as banking or insurance, have included additional variables that characterize the salient economic determinants of accruals specific to the industry with reasonable success.

It is important to keep in mind that the partition of total accruals into nondiscretionary and discretionary components is an estimate, and there are numerous things that could affect the estimates. Additionally, there are a number of ways one might go about estimating the coefficients b_0, b_1, and b_2. We may use all data for all firms from an estimation period that precedes the period in which we wish to estimate discretionary accruals ('pooled cross-sectional' estimation). A limitation of this method is that the coefficient estimates will be affected by differences in the economics across firms, and also by changes in the relation between total accruals, revenues, and PP&E through time. Alternatively, we might estimate firm-specific coefficients by just using data for a single firm during an estimation period. The benefit is that the relation between total accruals, revenues, and PP&E is likely fairly homogeneous across the estimation period, because we are focusing on a single firm. However, the downside is a loss of statistical power in the estimations, due to limited availability of a long time-series of data for a given firm. As a compromise, most researchers estimate the coefficients separately for different industries. Doing so reaches a compromise between the problems of a small sample size in firm-specific estimates and the 'averaging out' of differences that occurs with pooled cross-sectional estimates.

Evidence

Academic research has actively pursued the detection of earnings management for over three decades. However, there is surprisingly little evidence of earnings management. This lack of evidence has largely been attributed to a number of methodological shortcomings, but few have concluded that the lack of evidence indicates that earnings management does not occur. In other words, the maintained assumption among academics seems to reflect the opinions of those in practice.

What follows is a brief summary of various analyses that have been carried out over the years, and the general takeaways from the research. For tractability, the evidence is organized into subcategories relating to specific accounts, contractual terms, and corporate events that are examined, although several papers overlap these categories. Also, we conclude with a category relating to overall distributions of earnings, which has become the rallying point for renewed interest in earnings management. The interested reader should consult the references to obtain a more comprehensive discussion of the methodologies used, the firms investigated, and, perhaps most important, discussions of the numerous related papers not discussed here.

Specific accounts

One-time write-offs

The 'big bath' phenomenon is one where a manager faced with poor reported results decides to 'clean house' and write-down assets, accrue for estimated future costs, or record restructuring charges, driving reported performance even lower. Supposedly, the objective is to have investors or other important constituents of the firm ignore the large charge as transitory. Skeptics have suggested that managers are aggressive with these charges, which result in lower reported expenses in the future (for example, no depreciation for assets written down, no expenses for items accrued for in the one-time charge, and the like).

Researchers have documented some evidence that one-time write-offs appear to be used strategically by managers.

Deferred tax asset valuation allowance

Under current accounting standards, managers must estimate whether deferred tax assets recorded on the books might expire unused, due to a lack of reported taxable income in the future. A number of studies examine whether managers use the discretion over this estimate, but find no convincing evidence that they do.

Loan loss reserves of banks

A primary revenue-generating asset of commercial banks is a loan portfolio. Similar to accounts receivable, accounting rules encourage management to provide an allowance for uncollectible balances, referred to as a 'loan loss reserve' in banking. A number of researchers have documented relatively strong evidence of discretionary behavior in estimating the loan loss reserve. It is argued that managers exercise discretion to reduce the scrutiny of regulators, minimize taxes, or influence investor perceptions of the bank's value.

Claim loss reserves of insurance companies

The insurance industry provides a rich setting in which to investigate earnings management, due to certain regulatory disclosures that enable a researcher to assess management estimates (discretion) after the fact. 'Claim loss reserves' are management estimates of liabilities for incurred but not reported losses and claims. Similar to the loan loss reserves for banks, a number of studies have documented strong evidence of earnings management through these estimates.

Contracts

Bonus plans

Managers have a significant stake in reported earnings for a number of reasons, including bonus plans that are determined in part by the level of reported earnings. Academics have documented some evidence that managers exercise discretion to meet bonus plan thresholds, primarily through income-decreasing accruals when reported earnings would otherwise exceed minimum levels necessary for bonus plans (they 'save for the future'). However, there is some concern over the magnitude, robustness, or pervasiveness of such findings.

Debt covenants

Banks typically specify a number of accounting-based debt covenants that firms must adhere to in order to avoid being in technical default on a loan. Thus, managers have incentives to manipulate earnings when reported earnings are at a level that might trigger a violation of a covenant. Current evidence is mixed, and depends on what covenant is being examined.

Corporate events

Initial public offerings and seasoned equity offerings

Prior to an issuance of equity securities, managers have incentives to record income-increasing accruals to present a healthier financial condition and more optimistic expectations, yielding a higher offering price. Studies have found significant income-increasing accruals preceding equity offers.

Management buyouts

Firms going private provide a novel setting in which to investigate earnings management, because managers have incentives to manage earnings downwards prior to the tender offer in an attempt to depress the outstanding share price, making the acquisition of shares by the management team cheaper. Evidence in a few studies provides conflicting results, with one documenting no income-decreasing accruals in advance of a management buyout, and another documenting significant income-increasing accruals in the pre-buyout period.

Stock for stock mergers

In contrast to the incentives faced by management prior to a management buyout, managers contemplating an acquisition financed with the firm's stock have incentives to increase income prior to a tender offer to support a higher market valuation of the firm's stock. A higher valuation translates into fewer shares exchanged for the target's stock. Results document income-increasing accruals prior to an acquisition, and furthermore, that the amount of earnings measurement is related to the size of the acquisition (for example, larger benefits to earnings management).

Observed earnings distributions

Overall, the search for evidence of earnings management around specific corporate events and within specific accounts has resulted in somewhat mixed or weak evidence that managers manipulate earnings, with much of the evidence limited to a particular industry (for example, banks) or corporate event (for example, acquisition). Thus, one possible reason why evidence is somewhat mixed is that most of the studies focus on a small number of firms, which results in earnings management tests that have low power. In response to this, researchers have begun to look not at specific accounts or corporate events, but at overall distributions of earnings across large numbers of firms. By considering large numbers of firms, researchers are able to appeal to the 'law of large numbers' that suggests that many distributions tend to be normal (the bell-curve).

In these studies of earnings distributions, it is hypothesized that managers dislike reporting negative earnings, and will avoid reporting negative earnings if they have the opportunity to exercise discretion and bump earnings up to positive earnings. Also, it is hypothesized that managers would prefer to exercise discretion to manipulate earnings upwards, to avoid a decrease in reported earnings from an earlier fiscal quarter or year.

As an example of the results in these studies, we constructed Exhibit 7.3. It plots the distribution of earnings before extraordinary items scaled by market value for all firms from 1976 to 2000. Exhibit 7.3 presents the frequencies of reported earnings numbers (scaled by market value) for intervals of width 0.005 across the range –0.25 to +0.35. The overall shape of the distribution of earnings reflects the bell-curve that characterizes normal distributions. However, around earnings of zero, there is an unexplained kink in the distribution. There are fewer than expected frequencies of earnings just below zero, and more than expected frequencies of earnings just above zero. It appears that, barring some inexplicable property of earnings, managers who would have reported just slightly negative earnings intervened in the accounting process to produce earnings figures that were just above zero.

Exhibit 7.3

Distribution of earnings for all firms, 1976–2000

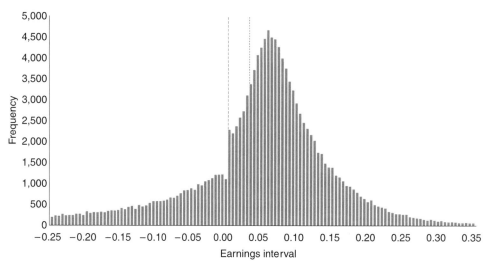

Source: Compustat.

What is the effect of pre-announcements?

In the days before earnings surprise was discussed on CNBC and available on web sites, there was little violent one day reaction of stock prices to earnings news. Since those times, 25% one day price movements in reaction to earnings announcements occur regularly. As corporate management does not enjoy large negative price movements, the practice of pre-announcements has become prevalent. Management hopes that by sharing potential negative news the price reaction to announcements would be more restrained. The following note from a brokerage firm would tend to confirm this view:

> Financial reporters must have had it relatively easy during this earnings season. They could prepare a boilerplate story and just fill in the specifics. 'XYZ Corp. reported earnings of ___ cents per share, a penny ahead of the lowered consensus forecast following the pre-announcement three weeks ago. However, the CEO of XYZ warned that difficult economic conditions and a strong dollar would continue to hurt results for the remainder of 2001. She suggested that sales for the second half would likely fall about 10% below current expectations, and she declined to forecast when conditions would improve.'[1]

Pre-announcements have quickly become part of the landscape. FirstCall has started collecting data on pre-announcements, and research is being done on the data. Research has been done subsequently to determine the effect of pre-announcements.

> Soffer, Thiagarajan and Walther found that firms with positive news only release some of this news at the pre-announcement date, while firms with negative news tend to release all of this news at the pre-announcement date. The decision to pre-announce magnifies the stock price

reaction to earnings surprises. Firms that pre-announce good (bad) news experience a greater positive (negative) excess return from the pre-announcement date to the earnings announcement date. So the question becomes 'Does the market efficiently incorporate the relation between the sign of the news at the pre-announcement date and the sign of the news at the earnings announcement date?' Buying those stocks with the most positive news or shorting those with the most negative news at the pre-announcement date yields an excess return of approximately 8% over 27 calendar days. They concluded that the market does not efficiently react to pre-announcements.[2]

Before investors paid attention to earnings surprises, there was no need to have pre-announcements. Earnings surprises were slowly reacted to by the marketplace, and did not have the dramatic effects they have today. Human nature being what it is, we modify our behavior to avoid pain. The pain of one day 30% price reductions has led senior management at companies to try to 'leak' bad information into the marketplace. This has led to the ever-increasing practice of pre-announcing bad news. It is a trend that will continue indefinitely. However, the good news for investors is that information appears to have a finite impact on the price of a stock, and that impact, in total, is the same whether a company pre-announces or not.

Summary

It is a widely held belief that managers manipulate accounting earnings. This belief underlies a large number of academic studies where researchers attempt to uncover evidence of earnings management. While there are a number of studies that provide evidence that is consistent with earnings management, those results are sometimes sensitive to the way earnings management is measured. Although many studies interpret their analysis as evidence of earnings management, a fair number lack evidence of earnings management. The closest evidence we have to a 'smoking gun' that earnings are managed is the analysis of overall distributions of earnings, which provides compelling evidence that managers avoid reporting slightly negative earnings or slightly decreasing earnings. This area remains interesting because of the unyielding belief that managers freely manipulate earnings.

References

Several summaries have been prepared that provided much of the background to this chapter. They include a full set of references to the most widely cited papers on earnings management:

Dechow, P., and D. Skinner (2000), 'Earnings Management: Reconciling the Views of Accounting Academics, Practitioners, and Regulators', *Accounting Horizons*, Vol. 15, No. 2, June.

Healy, P.M., and J.M. Wahlen (1999), 'A Review of the Earnings Management Literature and its Implications for Standard Setting', *Accounting Horizons*, Vol. 13, No. 4, December.

Schipper, K. (1989), 'Commentary on Earnings Management', *Accounting Horizons*, Vol. 3, No. 4, December.

In this chapter, we limited our definition of earnings management to what we termed 'classical' earnings management. We omitted discussion of several related areas, such as fraud, accounting choices, and operating decisions. The following papers and their included references address fraud through an analysis of Accounting and Auditing Enforcement Releases by the SEC:

Beneish, M.D. (1999), 'Incentives and Penalties Related to Earnings Overstatements that Violate GAAP', *The Accounting Review,* Vol. 74, No. 4, October, pp. 425–457.

Bonner, S.E., Z.V. Palmrose, and S.M. Young (1998), 'Fraud Type and Auditor Litigation: An Analysis of SEC Accounting and Auditing Enforcement Releases', *The Accounting Review,* Vol. 73, No. 4, October, pp. 503–532.

Dechow, P.M., R.G. Sloan, and A.P. Sweeney (1996), 'Causes and Consequences of Earnings Manipulation: An Analysis of Firms Subject to Enforcement Actions by the SEC', *Contemporary Accounting Research*, Spring, Vol. 13, No. 1, pp. 1–36.

Feroz, E.H., K. Park, and V.S. Pastena (1991), 'The Financial and Market Effects of the SEC's Accounting and Auditing Enforcement Releases', *Journal of Accounting Research,* Vol. 29, Supplement, pp. 107–142.

Additionally, the following summary papers discuss the evidence regarding management accounting method choices, and, to a lesser extent, operating decisions that impact reported income:

Fields, T.D., T.Z. Lys, and L. Vincent (2001), 'Empirical Research on Accounting Choice', *Journal of Accounting and Economics,* Vol. 31, Nos. 1–3, September, pp. 255–307.

Holthausen, R.W., and R.W. Leftwich (1983), 'The Economic Consequences of Accounting Choice – Implications for Costly Contracting and Monitoring', *Journal of Accounting and Economics,* Vol. 5, No. 2, pp. 77–117.

For an analytical model supporting the notion that current shareholders demand earnings management, see:

Dye, R. (1988), 'Earnings Management in an Overlapping Generations Model', *Journal of Accounting Research,* Vol. 26, pp. 195–235.

The Jones model and several of its subsequent modifications may be found in the following papers:

Dechow, P.M., R.G. Sloan, and A.P. Sweeney (1995), 'Detecting Earnings Management', *The Accounting Review*, Vol. 70, No. 2, April, pp. 193–225.

Jones, Jennifer (1991), 'Earnings Management During Import Relief Investigations', *Journal of Accounting Research,* Vol. 29, No. 2, pp. 193–228.

The following references are a very limited sampling of studies investigating specific accruals:

Ayers, B.C. (1998), 'Deferred Tax Accounting Under SFAS No. 109: An Empirical Investigation of its Incremental Value-Relevance Relative to APB No. 11', *The Accounting Review*, Vol. 73, No. 2, pp. 195–212.

Beatty, A., S. Chamberlain, and J. Magliolo (1995), 'Managing Financial Reports of Commercial Banks: The Influence of Taxes, Regulatory Capital and Earnings', *Journal of Accounting Research*, Vol. 33, No. 2, Autumn, pp. 231–261.

Beaver, W.H., and E.E. Engel (1996), 'Discretionary Behavior with Respect to Allowances for Loan Losses and the Behavior of Security Prices', *Journal of Accounting and Economics,* Vol. 22, Nos. 1–3, August-December, pp. 177–206.

Elliott, J.A., and J.D. Hanna (1996), 'Repeated Accounting Write-Offs and the Information Content of Earnings', *Journal of Accounting Research*, Vol. 34, pp. 135–155.

Francis, J., J.D. Hanna, and L. Vincent (1996), 'Causes and Effects of Discretionary Asset Write-Offs', *Journal of Accounting Research*, Vol. 34, pp. 117–134.

Miller, G.S., and D.J. Skinner (1998), 'Determinants of the Valuation Allowances for Deferred Tax Assets Under SFAS No. 109', *The Accounting Review*, Vol. 73, No. 2, pp. 213–233.

Petroni, K.R. (1992), 'Optimistic Reporting in the Property Casualty Insurance Industry,' *Journal of Accounting and Economics*, Vol. 15, pp. 485–508.

Petroni, K.R., S.G. Ryan, and J.M. Wahlen (2000), 'Discretionary and Non-Discretionary Revisions of Loss Reserves by Property-Casualty Insurers: Differential Implications for Future Profitability, Risk and Market Value', *Review of Accounting Studies*, Vol. 5, pp. 95–125.

These studies examine the manipulation of earnings in order to affect compensation:

Gaver, J., K. Gaver, and J. Austin (1995), 'Additional Evidence on Bonus Plans and Income Management', *Journal of Accounting and Economics*, Vol. 18, pp. 3–28.

Guidry, F., A. Leone, and S. Rock (1999), 'Earnings-Based Bonus Plans and Earnings Management by Business Unit Managers', *Journal of Accounting and Economics*, Vol. 26, January, pp. 113–142.

Healy, P. (1985), 'The Effect of Bonus Schemes on Accounting Decisions', *Journal of Accounting and Economics*, Vol. 7, pp. 85–107.

See the following studies for examinations of earnings management to avoid debt covenant violations:

DeFond, M.L., and J. Jiambalvo (1994), 'Debt Covenant Effects and the Manipulation of Accruals', *Journal of Accounting and Economics,* Vol. 17, January, pp. 145–176.

Healy, P., and K.G. Palepu (1990), 'Effectiveness of Accounting-Based Dividend Covenants', *Journal of Accounting and Economics,* Vol. 12, Nos. 1–3, pp. 97–124.

Incentives and results surrounding management buyouts are found in these papers:

DeAngelo, L. (1986), 'Accounting Numbers as Market Valuation Substitutes: A Study of Management Buyouts of Public Stockholders', *The Accounting Review*, Vol. 41, pp. 400–420.

Perry, S.E., and T.H. Williams (1994), 'Earnings Management Preceding Management Buyout Offers', *Journal of Accounting and Economics*, Vol. 18, No. 2, September, pp. 157–180.

Stock-for-stock acquisitions and the existence of earnings management is addressed in the following paper:

Erickson, M., and S. Wang (2000), 'Earnings Management by Acquiring Firms in Stock for Stock Mergers', *Journal of Accounting and Economics*, Vol. 27, No. 2, pp. 149–176.

To read more about the anomalous distributions of earnings and earnings changes, see the following papers:

Burgstahler, D., and I. Dichev (1997), 'Earnings Management to Avoid Earnings Decreases and Losses', *Journal of Accounting and Economics*, Vol. 24, No. 1, pp. 99–126.

DeGeorge, F., J. Patel, and R. Zeckhauser (1999), 'Earnings Management to Exceed Thresholds', *The Journal of Business*, Vol. 72, No. 1, January, pp. 1–33.

---

[1] Keon, Ed (2001), Equity Research, Prudential Securities, 30 July.

[2] Soffer, Leonard C., S. Ramuthiagarajan, and Beverley R. Walther (2003), 'Earnings Preannouncements', Working Paper.

Chapter 8

Accruals and earnings quality

Nothing is lasting that is feigned.

English proverb

In the chapters preceding this one, there has been a consideration of the uses of estimates of earnings. This chapter and the two that follow look in-depth at the earnings being estimated. There is a consideration of earnings quality, and then earnings management and pro forma earnings. This analysis will give investors a better idea of which earnings estimates have a greater likelihood of occurring and which do not.

Let us start with quality. Analysts forecast earnings, but it is cash flows that ultimately matter. There is a lot of misunderstanding about the link between earnings and cash flows. Simply stated, the difference between earnings and cash flows reflects accounting accruals. In this chapter, this link is briefly visited. Then, there is a discussion of how investors can take advantage of an understanding of this link to identify stocks that are likely to report earnings reversals.

The link between earnings and cash flows

To most people, the collective body of accounting rules known as U.S. Generally Accepted Accounting Principles (GAAP) is something that they know about but do not spend much time thinking about or talking about in public conversation. The goal of this set of rules, which becomes more voluminous and complex each year, is to provide a reporting system that is a better representation of the economic state of affairs and changes in the state of affairs of a company than we would get under a simpler reporting system.

The natural alternative is a cash basis method of reporting. Under a cash basis method of reporting, companies could conserve all kinds of resources by firing all the accountants, and just provide interested stakeholders a copy of annotated bank statements for the year. These bank statements enable outsiders to look at where the company got cash from and to whom it was sent. However, the volatility of cash flows would likely be quite high during periods of major purchases such as property, plant, or equipment. Similarly, large payments from customers would show up as big deposits, but perhaps the services or products paid for by the customers will not be provided for several months or years.

The goal of accrual accounting is to capture the impacts of cash events like these, but also events that may not necessarily involve cash in the current reporting period but nevertheless are important. The way that this is accomplished is through the use of accruals, which is a somewhat vague term reflecting any accounting entry recorded that does not reflect a current cash flow. Through the use of accruals, the cost of activities is matched to the periods that benefit.

For example, when a company buys a piece of machinery, the cost is clearly an asset. However, because things do not last forever, the machine will eventually wear out and will have to be replaced. The cost of the machine should be allocated or spread out over all the periods that the machine will be used to help the firm generate revenues. This is where we see the trade-off inherent in accrual accounting. The same machine could be used differently by two different companies, so there is generally not a 'standard' period that machines will benefit a company such that accounting rules might be written to specify the number of years different pieces of machinery will be useful. Consequently, there is a reliance on managers' estimates. We figure that managers are in the best position to estimate for how long the machine will be useful, and let them determine its 'useful life'. The cost of the machine is recorded as an expense a little bit at a time over the 'useful life' as the firm records depreciation expense. The act of recording the cost of the machine as an asset and then subsequently expensing the cost of the machine over a number of different periods is an example of accrual accounting.

Presumably, the use of accrual accounting results in financial reports that are more useful to investors who want to assess the timing and amounts of future cash flows. In fact, this is specifically emphasized in the Financial Accounting Standards Board (FASB) Statement of Financial Accounting Concepts No. 1, which is the 'bread and butter' conceptual framework that lists what accountants ought to be doing. There, the FASB states that:

> [F]inancial reporting should provide information to help investors, creditors, and others assess the amounts, timing, and uncertainty of prospective net cash inflows to the related enterprise (paragraph 37).

However, you might ask how accruals like depreciation recorded today help with predicting future cash flows. The key to understanding how accruals are useful is to think not of just a single accrual, but the overall effect of recording many accruals. There are accruals for revenues as well as for expenses. Together, it is hoped that the overall level of earnings reported is more useful than simply providing an annotated copy of a company's bank statement.

Accruals versus cash flows

How well does accrual accounting accomplish the objective of providing a better summary measure of performance than cash flows? Dechow (1994) studied the relative performance of cash flows and earnings at explaining stock returns. She first showed that as you lengthen the measurement interval, say several years, earnings and cash flows become more similar in their ability to measure a company's performance (that is, explain stock returns). This makes sense, because, over the life of a firm, the total earnings will equal the total cash flows. The key to her findings, however, is the analysis of earnings over shorter intervals, such as quarterly and annual earnings. For the shorter intervals, she shows that earnings dominate cash flows in their ability to explain stock returns. She concludes:

> [The results] demonstrate that cash flows are not a poor measure of firm performance *per se*. In steady-state firms, where the magnitude of accruals is small and cash flows and earnings are most similar, cash flows are a relatively useful measure of firm performance. However, when the magnitude of accruals increases, indicating that the firm has large changes in its operating, investment, and financing activities, cash flows suffer more severely from timing and matching problems. Therefore, as accruals increase in magnitude net cash flows' associ-

ation with stock returns declines. Overall, the results are consistent with the hypothesis that accountants accrue revenues and match expenditures to revenues so as to produce a performance measure (earnings) that better reflects firm performance than realized cash flows.

The evidence is compelling in favor of accrual accounting, and it is consistent with what we observe when we see analysts predominantly forecasting earnings rather than cash flows.

Accounting numbers as a measure of performance

Even though accrual accounting leads to financial reports that provide better summary information than would a cash-flow based report, accruals can be too much of a good thing. That is, rather than accruals providing enhanced earnings figures, they do the opposite.

At the Harvard Business School, the core accounting class emphasizes that the best accounting can do is provide a picture of a company's true economics, but that discretion available in accounting rules makes accounting numbers fuzzy. As a heuristic for communicating this idea in class, the following representative formula is used:

Accounting numbers = Economic substance + Measurement error + Bias

The formula is suggestive rather than an attempt to partition accounting numbers into separate quantities. Accounting numbers constitute any of the numbers from any of the financial statements, but the most common number is earnings. Economic substance is what accountants are trying to measure. For example, did a company generate value for its investors? Clearly, accountants would prefer that all accounting numbers reflect economic substance.

However, because accrual accounting requires that estimates be made (for example, the estimated life of a machine, its expected salvage value, and the like), the resulting accounting numbers will often be wrong, reflecting misestimates. This 'noise' in the accounting numbers is labeled measurement error. Some measurement error is expected and tolerable, but the hope is that overestimates from one period will be offset by small underestimates from another period, leading to just a small amount of measurement error.

Unfortunately, because managers are aware that accountants and financial statement users understand and tolerate some measurement error, they turn this to their advantage. Rather than provide estimates that increase the correspondence between accounting numbers and economic substance, dubious managers with incentives to overstate accounting numbers can infuse bias into those numbers. For example, managers can intentionally overestimate the useful lives of machinery, resulting in lower periodic depreciation charges.

This bias cannot go on forever because of the disciplined nature of double-entry accrual accounting. If a manager intentionally overstated the useful life of a machine, then the lower depreciation expense would result in an asset that is likely overstated. When the firm sells or disposes of the asset, it will likely record a loss on the sale or disposal. Such a loss is the 'catch-up' for the under-depreciation that resulted from the manager's intentional bias.

Another source of bias is actually built into accounting by accountants themselves. Despite the fact that the FASB does not actively seek conservative accounting methods, most of the rules that it issues are inherently biased towards being conservative (for example, recognizing unrealized losses but not unrealized gains). Thus, the conservative nature of accounting rules serves as an additional source of bias. If it is generally believed that managers have incentives to bias accounting numbers upwards, then the conservative nature of accounting rules provides some offset.

Accruals are sometimes not so good

The subjective nature of accruals recorded by managers makes them a dangerous thing. If managers are upstanding and transparent, then accruals enhance the financial statements' ability to convey the economic condition and performance of the firm. If, however, managers have less than noble objectives, then accruals are an easy to use tool to artificially modify the financial reports in some desired direction (usually up). There is a detailed discussion of this in the next chapter.

By way of introduction, in this chapter we want to simply visit accounting accruals from the perspective of their time-series behavior. It is useful to consider a simple example to appreciate further how accruals work.

Consider a simple sale of US$100,000 to be booked by a company. A customer places an order for products, and the company ships them to the customer. The customer receives them, and agrees to pay for the products within 30 days. Even though the accountant sees no cash coming in the door, the financial statements are nevertheless adjusted to reflect this transaction. In other words, accrual accounting is employed to better reflect the economic substance of the sale of products to a customer.

The accountant would record an account receivable asset for the amount that the customer owes the company, and would also go ahead and recognize the sales revenue for the sale of the products. The increase in the accounts receivable asset goes on the balance sheet, and will stay there until the customer pays off their account.

Suppose further that nothing else happened during this year. The increase in accounts receivable represents an 'income increasing' accrual. Nothing is wrong with income-increasing accruals per se. However, a small dose of healthy skepticism will trigger a concern that unscrupulous managers might abuse their discretion. In a real company, there is not just one sales transaction per year, but often thousands. With all the transactions, what is to keep a manager from bumping up the amount recorded as sales by some artificial amount? Auditors come in at the end of the year and spot check transactions recorded by managers, but they cannot view all transactions. As it turns out, most of the Accounting Enforcement Actions issued by the Securities and Exchange Commission (SEC), in which companies are admonished for fraudulent accounting, reveal that fictitious or overstated sales are usually behind the violation.

Note that we are not arguing that all managers 'bump up' the amount of revenues beyond that which is justified. Instead, we wish to provide a simple exposition of how accruals impose discipline on managers through the reversing process. To that end, we are introducing the possibility that accruals might be recorded at the wrong amounts initially, but this will work its way back out of the accounting system eventually.

To provide a contrasting example to the account receivable accrual, suppose also that the company discussed above rewards its sales staff with paid vacations in the year following a big sale, and that the sales agent who made the US$100,000 sale gets vacation time during which the company pays her US$1,000. The company would record the cost of this paid vacation in the current period during which the sale was recorded. This would require the company to record an expense and a corresponding accrued vacation liability. This is an example of an 'income decreasing' accrual.

Neither the income increasing nor the income decreasing accruals can continue indefinitely. They eventually reverse when the company either collects the account receivable or pays the employee her vacation time. However, over short periods of time, it should be clear that managers could do too much for income increasing accruals and too little for income decreasing accruals.

Now back to the sales example. Suppose that the manager decided to record the sale at US$120,000 rather than US$100,000. Eventually, the customer will pay, but will only pay what was invoiced to them (US$100,000). This leaves an uncollectible US$20,000 account receivable on the books. Sooner or later, the manager will have to clean out that receivable. To make things simple, suppose that when the manager writes off the bogus account receivable they have to record some kind of 'loss.' The loss decreases earnings in the period recorded. Plus, the amount of the loss is exactly equal to the amount by which sales were initially 'overbooked.' It is important to again restate that we do not mean to imply that the over booking of revenues or the under booking of expenses is routine.

Thus, if a manager overbooked revenue in the first year, leading to an overstatement of income in that year, the undoing of that overbooked revenue would come in the second year when the useless account receivable had to be written off. This provides a stylized example of a basic fact: all else equal, income increasing accruals in one period are generally followed by reversals in later periods. Similarly, income decreasing accruals in one period are generally followed by reversals in later periods.

Where to look

How is an investor to keep track of accruals made by managers? Fortunately, the statement of cash flows provides an investor with such information summarized nicely. For example, contrast the two excerpts from the operating section of the cash flow statements of Ebay and E-trade in Exhibits 8.1 and 8.2.

The operating section of the cash flow statement reconciles net income to cash flows from operating activities. The reconciling items reflect accruals recorded under GAAP. For Ebay, the reconciling items indicate a predominance of income-decreasing activities, because the net of the adjustments is positive. In contrast, for 1999 and 2001, the net adjustments for E-trade are negative, indicating that accounting accruals during those years were, on average, income

Exhibit 8.1

Ebay cash flow, 1999–2001 (US$)

	2001	2000	1999
Net income	90,448,000	48,294,000	10,828,000
Depreciation	89,732,000	45,191,000	25,331,000
Adjustments to net income	113,023,000	54,245,000	6,522,000
Changes in accounts receivables	(50,221,000)	(48,862,000)	(28,884,000)
Changes in liabilities	2,310,000	42,055,000	68,103,000
Changes in other operating activities	6,820,000	(40,775,000)	(15,336,000)
Cash flows from operating activities	252,112,000	100,148,000	66,564,000

Source: Authors' own.

Exhibit 8.2

E-trade cash flow, 1999–2000 (US$)

	2001	*2000*	*1999*
Net income	(241,532,000)	1,353,000	19,152,000
Depreciation	188,268,000	N/A	97,638,000
Adjustments to net income	(241,495,000)	N/A	(140,719,000)
Changes in accounts receivables	N/A	N/A	(3,586,689,000)
Changes in liabilities	20,738,000	N/A	3,306,275,000
Changes in other operating activities	19,327,000	N/A	165,651,000
Cash flows from operating activities	(254,694,000)	40,911,000	(138,692,000)

Source: Authors' own.

increasing. These two companies are symbolic of an average phenomenon that characterizes the behavior of future earnings conditional on accruals, which is discussed next.

Accruals and earnings behavior

Sloan (1996) investigated the time-series properties of earnings unconditionally, and conditional on the level of accruals embedded in earnings in the base year. He found that extreme earnings that contain a large amount of income increasing accruals tend to revert towards lower levels in the future years at a much quicker rate than extreme earnings unconditionally revert. However, extreme earnings levels that contain a disproportionately low level of income increasing accruals (which is another way of saying the earnings reflect a high level of cash flows) persist for longer periods before reverting.

Exhibit 8.3 was constructed based on net income scaled by total assets (ROA). We ranked firms into deciles according to ROA, then tracked ROA in the years prior to and after the ranking period.

Exhibit 8.3 demonstrates the well known mean reversion in earnings levels. Exhibit 8.4 was similarly constructed and tracks the level of ROA as well. However, in period $t = 0$, the ranking variable was accruals scaled by total assets, not net income scaled by total assets.

Clearly, the rate of mean reversion in earnings for extreme levels of accruals is much greater. This is a manifestation of the reversing nature of accounting accruals discussed in the stylized examples earlier.

Another way to construct the figure is to initially rank on the level of cash flows scaled by assets and track the mean reversion in levels of earnings (see Exhibit 8.5).

Exhibit 8.5 provides complementary evidence to Exhibit 8.4. However, when extreme levels of earnings are largely supported by underlying cash flows, the earnings levels, although reverting on average, tend to revert at a much slower rate than earnings that largely reflect accounting accruals.

Sloan (1996) documented that the stock market apparently does not appreciate these patterns in earnings. Exhibit 8.6 covers the period 1988–98 and reflects annual raw returns, value-weighted market adjusted returns, and size-decile adjusted returns for the three years subsequent to a portfolio formation year, across deciles formed on the basis of the level of accruals (for example, as in Exhibit 8.4).

Exhibit 8.3

Mean reversion effect

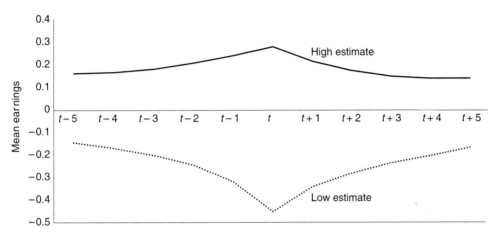

Source: Authors' own.

Exhibit 8.4

Accrual effect

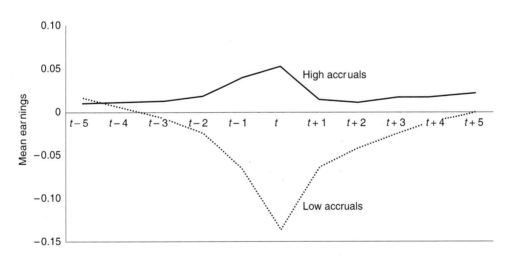

Source: Authors' own.

Exhibit 8.6 replicates the original findings of Sloan. Companies reporting high levels of accruals in a base year realize substantially lower returns in the following two years. On the other hand, companies with the lowest levels of accruals realize substantially higher levels of accruals in the subsequent two years. Together, these observed patterns in stock returns suggest a market that is either pleasantly or unpleasantly surprised when subsequent earnings either increase (after low and typically income decreasing accruals) or decrease (after high and typically income increasing accruals).

Exhibit 8.5

Cash flow effect

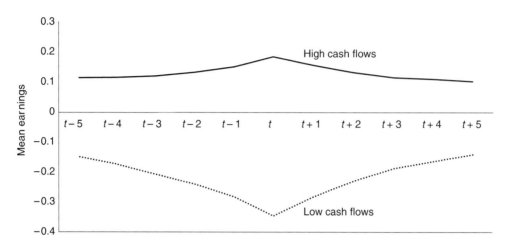

Source: Authors' own.

Exhibit 8.6

Returns for three-year periods across deciles 1988–98

	Raw returns			Market-adjusted returns			Size-adjusted returns		
Rank	$t + 1$	$t + 2$	$t + 3$	$t + 1$	$t + 2$	$t + 3$	$t + 1$	$t + 2$	$t + 3$
Low	0.203	0.249	0.217	0.037	0.076	0.038	0.048	0.073	0.025
2	0.211	0.229	0.235	0.049	0.060	0.060	0.064	0.065	0.048
3	0.183	0.185	0.227	0.022	0.018	0.056	0.038	0.021	0.049
4	0.161	0.165	0.187	−0.002	0.000	0.019	0.010	0.006	0.017
5	0.141	0.158	0.176	−0.019	−0.009	0.007	−0.002	−0.001	0.004
6	0.154	0.173	0.153	−0.006	0.006	−0.018	0.013	0.017	−0.025
7	0.152	0.175	0.213	−0.009	0.008	0.038	0.011	0.016	0.036
8	0.146	0.192	0.185	−0.017	0.024	0.012	0.000	0.033	0.010
9	0.117	0.149	0.219	−0.047	−0.017	0.041	−0.031	−0.012	0.033
High	0.080	0.147	0.210	−0.082	−0.023	0.034	−0.063	−0.018	0.025
N^c	35,956	28,608	22,429	35,956	28,608	22,429	35,107	27,951	21,932

Source: Authors' own.

The market seems to under-appreciate accruals, but do analysts?

One explanation for the observed patters of returns subsequent to extreme levels of accruals is that they are commensurate with compensation for risk. Even though the returns patterns noted above are robust to numerous methods of controlling for risk, it is still possible that those returns are merely compensation for some as of yet unidentified risk factor.

Exhibit 8.7

Earnings walkdown

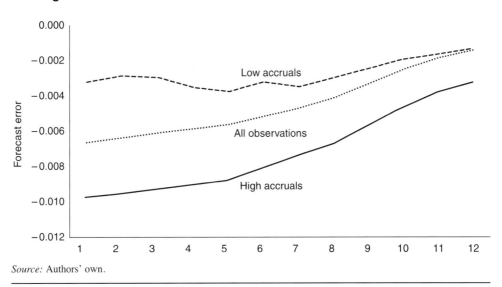

Source: Authors' own.

An alternative to examining stock returns is to examine analysts' forecasts around periods of extreme accruals. Examining analysts' forecasts does not require adjustment for risk, because the variable of interest is a forecast error. Bradshaw, Richardson, and Sloan (2001) investigated whether analysts understand the average reversion in earnings levels accompanied by extreme levels of accruals.

What they found was that analysts do not appear to understand the mean reversion either. Exhibit 8.7 tracks the average error in the consensus analyst forecast during the 12 months after a base year's earnings were reported. Exhibit 8.7 plots the average forecast error for the lowest and highest accruals deciles, as well as the average forecast error. The horizontal axis lists the number of months since the announcement of last year's results. The vertical axis reflects forecast error, scaled by stock price.

Exhibit 8.7 shows the walkdown in earnings that typically occurs and the average optimism in analysts' forecasts (forecast error = earnings – forecast, values less than zero indicate average optimism). Early on in a company's fiscal year, the analysts' forecasts are quite high, but they are gradually walked down presumably as analysts observe quarterly earnings announcements and receive 'guidance' from managers.

The forecast error for the high accrual decile is larger than the sample average and the forecast error for the low accrual decile for all months. This pattern suggests that analysts do not initially anticipate the fact that high accruals last year generally indicate quick earnings reversion (declines) in the current year, or that low accruals in the last year generally indicate earnings turnarounds. However, analysts do seem to pick up on this pattern during the year.

Summary

The link between accruals and earnings is a useful aspect of the financial reporting system to understand. Although there is some evidence that analysts pick up on this link, the adjustments made by them are slow and incomplete, on average. This provides savvy investors with an opportunity to improve upon the consensus forecast by doing a little digging into the financial statements.

References

Accruals versus cash flows:

Dechow, P.M. (1994), 'Accounting Earnings and Cash Flows as Measures of Firm Performance: The Role of Accounting Accruals', *Journal of Accounting and Economics,* Vol. 18, No. 1, pp. 3–42.

Accruals:

Bradshaw, M.T., S.A. Richardson, and R.G. Sloan (2001), 'Do Analysts and Auditors Use Information in Accruals?', *Journal of Accounting Research*, Vol. 39, No. 1, June, pp. 45–74.

Sloan, R.G. (1996), 'Do Stock Prices Fully Reflect Information in Accruals and Cash Flows about Future Earnings?', *The Accounting Review,* Vol. 71, No. 3, July, pp. 289–315.

Chapter 9

Whisper estimates

It isn't what they say about you, it's what they whisper.

Errol Flynn

Up to this point, this book has focused on the estimates made by analysts that are sent to the data collectors (for instance, FirstCall, I/B/E/S, Multex and Zacks). What about estimates of future earnings that are generated but are not collected by the data services? Does finding them and using them provide any informational advantage? We can examine this question by analyzing whisper estimates.

Whisper estimates became popular in the 1990s. They are the natural outgrowth of the behavioral adjustments that continually occur in the earnings estimate cycle. When estimates were first collected by I/B/E/S, there was no need to whisper. People barely paid attention to the published estimates. By the mid 1980s, use of estimates in managing institutional money began to proliferate. So when the technology bubble hit in the late 1990s, estimate data was so popular that it appeared on websites aimed at individual investors. When published estimates become common knowledge, the next step in the behavioral cycle is to try to get better or faster information than the estimate. This led to the growth of whisper estimates. Whisper forecasts of quarterly earnings per share (EPS) are unofficial forecasts that are passed among Wall Street professionals and now also on internet sites. Whisper forecasts are what analysts share with clients on an unofficial basis. These forecasts can be based on incomplete information or recent news. Thus, the impression among Wall Street professionals was that whisper forecasts were more accurate expectations of earnings than consensus analyst forecasts published by major forecast tracking services (for example, IBES/First Call and Zacks). The notion of higher accuracy comes from the fact that actual earnings can be different from expectations, due to the cushion arising from the manager's desire to be conservative in setting expectations for Wall Street analysts. The whisper estimates, supposedly, bridge this gap and provide more accurate forecasts.

What are whisper numbers?

Whisper numbers are alternative measures of earnings expectations. They are informal forecasts that differ from the consensus estimates created when companies provide guidance to Wall Street analysts, who then issue earnings estimates. As the date of the actual earnings announcement approaches, an identifiable shift in earnings expectations emerges. Many observers attribute this shift to momentum generated by industry competitors, earnings revisions by analysts behind closed doors, and investor 'word of mouth', which can and do affect overall market sentiment. From Kipplinger.com this additional estimate of profits is thought to represent what an analyst really thinks a company will earn in a given quarter. An analyst will relay his whisper number to his firm's larger clients (generally mutual and pension funds). Individuals can get whisper numbers from websites including EarningsWhispers.com WhisperNumber.com.

An example is WhisperNumber.com, which creates a whisper that is based on the expectations of the mass demographic of individual investor's for quarterly earnings and revenues. The estimates are the individual investor's expectations based on shared information, fundamental research, past earnings performance, 'gut feel', media, press release information, and corporate information.

Where do whisper number providers get their data?

The oldest service on the web, WhisperNumber.com, invites investors (both individual and professionals investors) with stock market ideas to submit their expectations on quarterly earnings to their site. WhisperNumber.com does not collect analyst data for earnings reports. WhisperNumber.com also claims to track every message on every stock of the four leading message boards to further search and reveal investor expectations and sentiment on earnings. The performance of this data is tracked and compared to the consensus number.

Before a number is submitted to their site, the numbers go through a stringent quality assurance program. Based on a series of checks and balances, their quality assurance processes have evolved into an automated and detailed system. They claim to have over 15 'red flag alerts' in place allowing for review of whisper entry and data collection. Examples include similar/multiple email address, similar/multiple IP address, significant activity on one stock, significant activity from one user, and significant activity in a specified time period. After the quality assurance process is complete, the aggregated number from the collection process is submitted to the site for publication.

Exhibits 9.1 and 9.2 show examples of information available at whisper web sites.

Exhibit 9.1

EarningsWhispers.com

Procter & Gamble Co	*$89.01*	*$0.00*	*0.00%*

1st Quarter Ending September 2002

		Trends	
Earnings Whisper®:	$1.10	Stock Price:	▼
Analysts' Estimate:	$1.09		
Members' Estimate:	N/A	Analysts' Target:	▲
Release Date:	10/29/02		
		Analysts' Estimate:	N/A
Analysts' Recommendation:	Buy		
Visitors' Sentiment:	Strong Buy	Visitors' Sentiment:	▲
		Analysts' Recommendation:	▼
Analysts' Target:	$101		
Members' Target:	$105	Earnings Surprises:	▲

Source: EarningsWhispers.com.

Exhibit 9.2
WhisperNumber.com

Company	Symbol	Consensus whisper number		Actual
Cisco	CSCO	0.09	0.10	0.11
Microsoft	MSFT	0.51	0.48	0.49
Sun Microsystems	SUNW	−0.02	−0.01	−0.01
JDS Uniphase	JDSU	−0.02	−0.03	−0.03
Dell Computer	DELL	0.16	0.17	0.17
AOL/Time Warner	AOL	0.13	0.17	0.18
Nokia Corporation	NOK	0.15	0.17	0.17
Motorola	MOT	−0.12	−0.09	−0.08
Home Depot	HD	0.33	0.34	0.36
Amazon	AMZN	−0.09	−0.02	−0.01
Harley Davidson	HDI	0.36	0.38	0.39
Ford	F	−0.15	−0.08	−0.06

Source: WhisperNumber.com.

Do academic studies support whisper estimates: supporting evidence

Bagnoli, Beneish, and Watts (2000) compared whisper estimates collected from web chat rooms to the First Call consensus. Much to their surprise, they found that the whisper estimates were closer to the reported EPS on average and did not have the same understated bias as the First Call consensus. They found that the First Call consensus tended to be more pessimistic and less accurate (about 6.1% below reported earnings per share), whereas the postings were 4.9% above the actual results. According to the abstract from their paper:

> First, we find that whisper forecasts are, on average, more accurate than First Call forecasts. Second, we find that First Call forecasts exhibit a pessimistic bias whereas whisper forecasts exhibit a slight optimistic bias. These results are consistent with the Street wisdom that analysts underestimate earnings and that whispers arise to 'undo' their underestimation. We further find that our whispers tend be associated with 'momentum' firms (firms that are younger and experiencing more rapid growth than control firms) and that the whispers themselves are marginally more highly associated with stock price reactions to quarterly earnings announcements. When considered collectively, our results suggest that whispers contain information not contained in First Call analyst forecasts and that this information is at least partly reflected in stock prices prior to the earnings release. The purpose of the paper is to compare unofficial forecasts of earnings known as 'whispers' to forecasts generated by First Call analysts. Our sample consists of approximately 900 whispers found primarily on message boards on investor web sites between 1995 and 1997. Our analysis yields the following results. First, whispers are, on average, more accurate than First Call forecasts, and they are better proxies for the market's expectation of the forthcoming earnings. Second, while First Call forecasts tend to underestimate earnings, on average, whispers tend to overestimate them. Finally, trading strategies based on the relation between whisper and First Call forecasts yield abnormal returns. This suggests that whispers contain information beyond that contained in analysts' forecasts and that the market impounds that information into price before earnings are announced.[1]

Indeed, First Call has produced 'hisper' (HIstorical SurPrise-based EaRnings) numbers for selected companies by adjusting the consensus forecasts to reflect recent earnings surprises. Bagnoli and Watts found that these 'hispers' were more accurate than the First Call consensus forecasts.

In other words, the market recognizes that corporations are managing earnings and expectations to small surprises, and adjusts analysts' forecasts to reflect this. However, how does one explain the year by year creep to larger and larger earnings surprises? Corporations, in order to keep ahead of the whisper estimates, must feel that they must produce larger and larger surprises relative to the analysts' consensus.

Do academic studies support whisper estimates: evidence to the contrary

A recent working paper by Rees and Adut (2002) examines whisper forecasts in a more recent time period. They investigate whether SEC's Regulation Fair Disclosure (Reg FD) has had any impact on the accuracy of analyst forecasts versus whisper forecasts. Using a sample covering the period 2000–01, they report that whisper forecasts are more accurate than analyst forecasts before Reg FD, but that analyst forecasts become more accurate than whispers after Reg FD. Also, contrary to Bagnoli et al. (1999), they report that analyst forecasts are a better proxy for the market expectations of earnings. However, this study uses only one website. We collect a comprehensive sample from multiple websites as well as from the financial press (via Lexis-Nexis). Also, our sample period of 1999–2001 encompasses both the economic 'boom' years as well as the initial period of the general economic downturn.

Thus, it seems that some fundamental changes took place since the sample period of the Bagnoli et al. (1999) study in how the whisper numbers are being generated and disseminated. Whisper estimates are no longer confined to high-tech sectors. Also, the variance of whisper estimates will likely increase, as individual investors are increasingly posting whisper forecasts. Consequently, it is timely and relevant to systematically study the characteristics and market perceptions of whisper numbers in more recent years. Anecdotal evidence states that, even though whisper estimates are popular with individual investors, they are not popular with institutional investors. Part of this is due to the lack of availability of the data on whisper estimates in a form that is readily useable for asset management. Perhaps more important is the reliability of these estimates. Whisper numbers have not generated very much interest in the institutional investment world, possibly due to the perception that whisper information has a high degree of noise. Consequently, vendors of forecast estimates, such as IBES/First Call and Zacks, have not attempted to compile and provide this information. However, no rigorous empirical evidence exists regarding the accuracy and value relevance of whisper estimates vis-à-vis analysts' consensus forecasts in more recent years. Therefore, we systematically analyze and document the characteristics and market perceptions of whisper estimates and analysts' consensus estimates, using a sample of 1,008 observations over the period 1999–2001.

Specifically, the following research question was examined by Bhattacharya, Sheikh, and Thiagarajan ('Does the Market Listen to Whispers?', submitted to the *Journal of Investing*, 2003): Are whisper forecasts more accurate than consensus analyst forecasts? This question seeks to answer whether whisper numbers better capture earnings expectations than consensus forecasts. This research question is capable of providing insights into the extent of sophisticated institutional investors' use of whisper numbers.

The results of their analysis suggest that whisper forecasts are generally more optimistic than consensus analyst forecasts. However, in contrast to Bagnoli et al. (1999), they find no evidence that whispers are more accurate than analyst forecasts. This is consistent with our expectations given the increased variability and noise inherent in whisper numbers. In terms

Exhibit 9.4

Comparison of accuracy between analysts' consensus estimate and whisper estimate

Panel A: Forecast errors scaled by price two days before the earnings announcement date

Subsample	N	Mean of absolute forecast errors based on consensus estimate (%)	Mean of absolute forecast errors based on whisper estimate (%)	Difference in means[1]	Median of absolute forecast errors based on consensus estimates (%)	Median of absolute forecast errors based on whisper estimates (%)	Difference in medians[2]
All forecast errors	1008	0.368	0.380	0.29 (0.768)	0.061	0.060	0.71 (0.476)
Whisper greater than consensus	630	0.279	0.304	0.58 (0.561)	0.057	0.050	0.97 (0.328)
Whisper less than consensus	172	0.828	0.842	0.10 (0.919)	0.174	0.293	2.68 (0.007)

Panel B: Forecast errors scaled by absolute actual earnings

Subsample	N	Mean of absolute forecast errors based on consensus estimate (%)	Mean of absolute forecast errors based on whisper estimate (%)	Difference in means	Median of absolute forecast errors based on consensus estimates (%)	Median of absolute forecast errors based on whisper estimates (%)	Difference in medians
All forecast errors	1008	28.40	27.90	0.21 (0.834)	9.09	9.09	0.08 (0.938)
Whisper greater than consensus	630	20.83	20.84	0.01 (0.995)	8.26	6.37	2.14 (0.032)
Whisper less than consensus	172	56.99	55.46	0.17 (0.863)	15.00	25.00	2.96 (0.003)

Notes:

[1] We use the parametric t test to determine the difference in means. The column reports t statistics and two-tailed probabilities in parentheses.

[2] We use the Wilcoxon sign-rank test to determine the difference in medians. The column reports Wilcoxon Z statistics and two-tailed probabilities in parentheses.

Source: Authors' own.

of market perception, they find that investors do not pay attention to whispers based on both short-window and long-window tests. In both the short-run and the long-run, whisper forecasts have no incremental information content over consensus analyst forecasts. Furthermore, they find no evidence that analysts revise their forecasts in light of the information contained in whispers. Overall, these results suggest that institutional investors do not pay much attention to whisper numbers.

The results are shown in Exhibit 9.4. In Exhibit 9.4, Panel A shows that the mean (median) forecast error based on consensus analyst forecasts is 0.368% (0.061%), while the mean (median) forecast error based on whisper forecasts is 0.380% (0.060%). These are not significantly different from each other. For the sub-sample where whisper forecasts are greater than consensus analyst forecasts, there is no significant difference in mean or median forecast errors. However, for the sub-sample where whisper forecasts are less than consensus forecasts, the median of absolute whisper forecast errors is significantly greater than the median of absolute consensus forecast errors (no significant difference in means), suggesting that whisper numbers are less accurate than consensus forecasts.

Panel B provides results very similar to the results reported in Panel A. They do not find significant difference between the accuracy of consensus and whisper forecasts except in two cases. In the sub-sample where whisper numbers are greater than consensus analyst forecasts, we find that the median absolute whisper forecast error is significantly smaller than the median absolute consensus forecast error, suggesting that whispers are more accurate than consensus forecasts. However, in the sub-sample where whisper numbers are less than consensus analyst forecasts, median absolute whisper forecast error is significantly greater than median absolute consensus forecast error, suggesting that whisper forecasts are less accurate. Overall, the results reported in Exhibit 9.4 do not provide any evidence that whisper forecast is more accurate, or provides a better expectation of earnings, than consensus analyst forecast.

Conclusion

As the technology bubble has collapsed, so has the focus on whisper estimates. Original research seemed to show that whisper estimates were slightly more accurate, but to date, no academic study has been able to conclusively prove that use of whisper estimates improves investment returns. Results of recent research indicate that whisper forecasts are more optimistic and generally greater than consensus analyst forecasts. However, we find no evidence that whispers are more accurate than analyst forecasts. In terms of market perception, we find that investors do not pay attention to whispers based on both short window and long window tests. In both the short run and the long run, whispers are not incrementally informative to the consensus analyst forecasts. In contrast, analysts' consensus forecasts often have incremental information content over whisper numbers. Also, there is no evidence that analysts revise their forecasts in light of the information contained in whispers. This body of evidence indicates that institutional or professional investors (those who most often move prices) do not pay much attention to whisper forecasts. No wonder, then, that the focus on whispers has faded among investors and Wall Street professionals.

References

Bagnoli, Mark, Messod D. Beneish, and Susan G. Watts (2000), 'Earnings Expectations: How

Important are the Whispers?', *American Association of Individual Investors Journal*, June, Vol. 22, No. 5, pp. 11–14.

Pulliam and Pettit (2000), Working Paper.

---

[1] Mark Bagnoli, Messod Daniel Beneish, and Susan G. Watts, 'Whisper Forecasts of Quarterly Earnings per Share', *Journal of Accounting & Economics*, Vol. 28, No. 1, August 1999. In light of the evidence that corporations are managing forecasts to small positive surprises, this does not seem like an unreasonable finding. It represents the market's reaction to earnings managed to positive surprises.

Chapter 10

Are there superior analysts?

It is wise to remember that too much success in the stock market is in itself an excellent warning.

Gerald Loeb

It has been have shown in the chapter on the role of analysts that analysts are, on average, 41% wrong. The key phrase is 'on average'. Are there better analysts? Do analysts at large firms, or who are Institutional Investor All-Americans, predict earnings any better than the average? Cynics will say that all analysts are so affected by conflicts of interest (as discussed in Chapter 4) that their research should be viewed with skepticism at best. However, surely there are at least some analysts who are pretty good at their job. Otherwise, wouldn't the costs of staffing a research department have outweighed any benefits, leading to the inevitable demise of the research function? The costs are nontrivial; in 1991, the *Wall Street Journal* reported an estimate of running a typical research department at US$40–50 million per year. In this chapter, there is a consideration of the evidence on the existence of superior analysts. As it turns out, depending on how you measure 'superior,' there do seem to be certain analysts who are better than others. There is also a consideration of research that concludes that not only does the market believe that there are superior analysts, but the market gives more weight to forecasts, recommendations, and target prices of superior analysts, resulting in stronger market reactions to their announcements.

Anecdotal evidence

How do you measure a 'superior' analyst? The first things that should come to mind are the accuracy of their earnings forecasts, and the profitability of their stock recommendations. These two measures are largely those that are commonly used.

Each year, there are a number of rankings of analysts that appear in the financial press. Two of the more popular are the *Institutional Investor* 'All-American Research Team' and the *Wall Street Journal* 'Best on the Street' rankings. Both rankings are based on a combination of individual analysts' forecast accuracy, recommendation profitability, and surveys of investor relations personnel. Unless certain analysts repeatedly show up on the rankings, we might just view the rankings as the manifestation of chance. This would be consistent with the results of another ranking done by the *Wall Street Journal*, the 'Dartboard' column, which was retired in 2002 after a 14 year run.

In the Dartboard feature, several analysts were asked to select stocks, and their investment performance was tracked against a matched sample of stocks selected by means of darts thrown at the stock quotes pages of the *Wall Street Journal*. Over the course of this 'competition,' the professionals racked up an average gain of approximately 10.2% six-month gain versus 3.5% for the darts and 5.6% for the Dow. These results would appear to suggest that professionals definitely possess skill at selecting stocks. However, despite validation by academics, the Dartboard analysis was hardly a rigorous basis for writing off the notion that there are indeed superior analysts. A glaring problem with this comparison was that professionals given just one or two opportunities to participate in the column might be inclined to 'swing for the fence', and select a number of highly risky, speculative stocks. This could be one explanation for their superior return. Another possibility is causality. It is possible that the publicity effect of being picked by a professional would induce price pressure in the subject stock, which could also explain some of the superior returns of the professionals.

What about such factors as timeliness or frequency? Recently, several commercial data providers have initiated information services that report or rely on differential earnings forecast accuracy across analysts. StarMine is a subscriber service that has done weighting calculations based on determinants of forecast accuracy. They calculate a proprietary consensus forecast that, they argue, is superior to the standard consensus calculation done by such analyst data clearinghouses as First Call, where the consensus is a simple equally weighted average of all outstanding earnings forecasts.

Most of the focus on weighting superior analysts' forecasts is recent. Previously, the belief that there were analysts whose forecasts were consistently more accurate, or whose recommendations were persistently more profitable, was not widely held, or perhaps the technology was not refined enough to identify superior analysts.

The evidence

Most of the evidence on differential abilities across analysts focuses on their ability to forecast earnings. Accordingly, most of our discussion is devoted to earnings forecasts. However, later the results of new research is noted that examines analysts' other outputs for evidence of persistent superior abilities.

The initial research on analyst forecasts followed a long series of studies that examined the ability of time-series models to predict earnings. These models utilize statistical models that are used to estimate coefficients on various parameters during an estimation period. The estimated coefficients are then applied to current data to come up with a forecast of future earnings. For example, assume that we believe that a company's quarterly earnings can be represented by the following equation:

$$X_t = X_{t-4} + \phi_1 (X_{t-1} - X_{t-5}) + \varepsilon$$

Here, quarterly earnings are represented by the Xs and the subscripts refer to quarters. This model (which is an 'AR(1) model in seasonal differences') says that we expect earnings in quarter t to be equal to the earnings from the same quarter one year ago ($t-4$) plus some fraction (ϕ_1, between zero and one) of last quarter's change in seasonal quarterly earnings ($X_{t-1}-X_{t-5}$). We would gather a bunch of data for some period of time, say 1990–99, and estimate the coefficient ϕ_1. Then, to forecast earnings for, say, the first quarter of 2000, we would need actual earnings from last quarter, four quarters ago, and five quarters ago. Then, we would simply add X_{t-4} and the product of ϕ_1 times ($X_{t-1}-X_{t-5}$) to arrive at the estimate of first quarter earnings for 2000. Clearly, this procedure requires that we have a sufficient number of past observations in order to estimate ϕ_1 and it is objective. However, it potentially ignores all kinds of information that is available regarding product markets, industry conditions, competitive threats, and so on. It stands to reason, then, that any human might be able to use this other information, and even information from time-series models, to come up with better predictions of earnings than relying solely on a time-series model. Furthermore, it also stands to reason that some humans are better than others at translating all of this information into better earnings forecasts.

This was the line of inquiry that first led to the examination of properties of analysts' forecasts. Early studies provided relatively straightforward evidence that analysts provided more accurate forecasts than state-of-the-art time-series models. A simple explanation for analysts' superiority over time-series models is a timing advantage. In contrast to time-series forecasts, which use only information in reported earnings up to a recent time period, analysts are able to use additional information not in prior reported earnings, and also information that became available since the ending period of the data used in the time-series forecasts. Not surprisingly, even after controlling for the timing advantage analysts have relative to time-series forecasts, analysts provide more accurate forecasts of earnings, on average.

Following the 'horse races' between analysts' forecasts and time-series models, research began examining forecasts of individual analysts relative to each other. For a long time, academic research failed to demonstrate the existence of superior earnings forecasters. The earliest evidence modeled earnings forecast accuracy as a function of analyst, firm, and time period fixed effects. For example, forecast accuracy was defined as the absolute value of the difference between the actual earnings (X) and the analyst's forecast (F). With a sample of i analysts, j firms, and t years, one would have estimated the following model:

$$|E_{i,j,t} - F_{i,j,t}| = \sum_{i=1}^{I} \alpha_i ANALYST_i + \sum_{j=1}^{J} \beta_j FIRM_j + \sum_{t=1}^{T} \gamma_t TIME_t$$

where $ANALYST_i$ is an indicator variable for the i'th analyst, $FIRM_j$ is an indicator variable for the j'th firm, and $TIME_t$ is an indicator variable for time period t. An F-test for collective significant explanatory power of the α coefficients provided evidence for whether there was a significant analyst-specific component of earnings forecast errors. Early research found insignificant results, and concluded that analysts did not exhibit systematic differential abilities at forecasting earnings.

The above specification for testing individual analyst ability was state of the art up until the early 1990s. At that time, researchers began to refine the specification of analyst forecast errors to include controls for the recency of the forecast. As in the early research that compared analysts to time-series models, comparisons of individual analyst forecasts are subject to the contaminating impact of timing advantages. Clearly, an analyst who makes a forecast just one month prior to an annual earnings announcement will have an informational advantage over an analyst (perhaps the same analyst) who makes a forecast, say, 11 months prior to the announcement of annual earnings. Indeed, it was this very reason that researchers attributed the superiority of analysts' forecasts over time-series forecasts that were all the rage in the 1970s and 1980s. In other words, it was not really fair to compare forecasts made at different points in time, because the most recent forecast has an unfair advantage due to information that became available between the time of the earlier forecast and the time of the most recent forecast.

To examine differences in analysts, researchers obtain individual forecasts across firms and time. It is customary to retain forecasts released during some prespecified time frame, for example, between five and 20 trading days prior to the fiscal quarter end being forecasted. Then, forecast errors are calculated for each forecast as follows:

$$FE_{ijt} = F_{ijt} - X_{ijt}$$

where FE is forecast error, F is the individual analyst forecast of earnings per share, and X is the actual reported earnings per share. The subscripts refer to analyst i, firm j, and time period t. After calculating forecast errors, the forecast errors are used to compute an individual analyst specific average forecast error. This can be done with simple ordinary least squares regressions similar to the equation listed above regarding aggregate analyst effects:

$$|FE_{ijt}| = ANALYST_i + FIRM_j + TIME_t + \varepsilon_{ijt}$$

Here, we are concerned with the average level of accuracy of an analyst's forecasts, hence we take the absolute value of the forecast error. Signed forecast errors can be analyzed as well, and are typically thought of as 'bias' rather than 'accuracy.' The primary variables of interest are the residual terms, ε_{ijt}. Basing inferences on individual analyst forecast errors on this equation alone, researchers conclude that there is no difference in analyst accuracy. However, as alluded to above, this is because the forecasts typically have varying degrees of recency. Further controls for recency of the forecast are obtained by examining the above equation after restricting attention to forecasts approximately of the same age.

Another method to compare individual analysts against each other is to form matched samples of analysts following the same firm at the same point in time. Results over a number of academic studies demonstrate that these tests are high power and identify superior analysts.

What has the research shown?

Stickel (1992) did the first research that we are aware of in trying to answer the question of superior analysts. Up until his research, it was assumed that *Institutional Investor* All-American analysts were more accurate, as they had better access to companies than the average analyst. Being a member of the All-American research team was viewed in the study as a proxy for relative reputation and compensation. Stickel showed that returns immediately following large upward forecast revisions favored the idea that leading analysts might have a bigger impact on stock prices. However, there was virtually no difference in returns following downward revisions. This unusual finding provided no conclusive evidence that All-Americans were superior to other analysts.

StarMine Corporation has recently started providing data on more accurate analysts and trying to create more accurate forecasts. StarMine provides different metrics to predict earnings: their AccurateAnalysts product overweights estimates from historically accurate analysts; Clusters identifies groups of recent revisions, and excludes older estimates; their ExperiencedAnalysts product overweights estimates from analysts with long track records on a stock; and their TopBrokers product uses only estimates from the 15 largest brokerages.

Additional work continues to be done on ways to find more accurate analysts. One recent theory from Andrew Rudd at BARRA suggests that analysts at larger firms are leaders and smaller firms are followers. The theory suggests that large firms have more resources available to analysts, and allow analysts to cover fewer securities than smaller regional brokerage firms. These resources allow them to cover companies more thoroughly and react to information that comes in the marketplace more quickly. This combination, in theory, should allow them to perform better than firms that are less timely and have less resources.

Summary

Contrary to the criticism that analysts are merely puppets of management, there is ample evidence that some analysts are better than others. This is both comforting and disturbing to investors who use analysts' forecasts and recommendations in their own personal investment decisions. It is comforting to know that some analysts are experts, as they should be. However, it is disturbing insofar as an investor is probably unsure as to the quality of forecasts and recommendations of all but only a handful of analysts that tend to receive the most acclaim in the annual analyst rankings.

Further reading

Read about the final *Wall Street Journal* 'Dartboard' column in 'Journal's Dartboard Retires After 14 Years of Stock Picks', 18 April 2002.

For early evidence that concluded there appeared to be no differences in analysts' abilities to forecast earnings, see:

Butler, K.C., and L.H.P. Lang (1991), 'The Forecast Accuracy of Individual Analysts: Evidence of Systematic Optimism and Pessimism', *Journal of Accounting Research*, pp. 150–156.

O'Brien, P. (1990), 'Forecast Accuracy of Individual Analysts in Nine Industries', *Journal of Accounting Research*, Vol 28, pp. 286–304.

More recent evidence that refined methodologies, and controlled for forecast recency and examinations of outputs other than earnings forecasts, include:

Bradshaw, M.T., and L.D. Brown (2002), 'An Examination of Sell-Side Analysts' Abilities to Predict Target Prices', Working Paper, Harvard Business School and Georgia State University.

Mikhail, M.B., B.R. Walther, and R.H. Willis (2002), 'Do Security Analysts Exhibit Persistent Differences in Stock Picking Ability?', Working Paper, Duke University and Northwestern University.

Sinha, P., L.D. Brown, and S. Das (1997), 'A Re-Examination of Financial Analysts' Differential Earnings Forecast Accuracy', *Contemporary Accounting Research*, Vol 14, pp. 1–42.

Stickel, S. (1992), 'Reputation and Performance Among Security Analysts', *Journal of Finance*, Vol 47, pp. 1811–1836.

Finally, the following is a sampling of papers investigating determinants of analyst superiority:

Clement, M.B. (1999), 'Analyst Forecast Accuracy: Do Ability, Resources, and Portfolio Complexity Matter?', *Journal of Accounting and Economics*, Vol. 27 No. 3, pp. 285–303.

Jacob, J., T.Z. Lys, and M.A. Neale (1999), 'Expertise in Forecasting Performance of Security Analysts', *Journal of Accounting and Economics*, Vol. 28, No. 1, pp. 51–82.

Mikhail, M., B. Walther, and R. Willis (1997), 'Do Security Analysts Improve their Performance with Experience?', *Journal of Accounting Research*, Vol. 35, pp. 131–166.

Chapter 11

Earnings revisions

All things must change to something new.

Henry Wadsworth Longfellow

So far there has been an examination of the history of earnings estimates, the role of analysts, and the use of estimate data in looking at earnings surprises. This chapter now focuses on another tool utilized by professional money managers: earnings revisions. As analyst data is not accurate, understanding revisions and the sentiment that they impart is of critical importance to investors.

Analyst revisions have been used by professional money managers for many years. Originally, portfolio managers would read the reports produced by analysts and those analyst's estimates of future earnings, and use the information in an non-structured way in making decisions. Perhaps the fact an analyst had a strong buy on the stock would be important to a portfolio manger. Or maybe it was information in the report about the solidity of the business model that would trigger a buy. The information gleaned from these reports was utilized best by looking at one or two analysts and drilling down in the reports for information. It was not until the advent of I/B/E/S that a large collection of analyst opinions was available from one source. This ability to get data from a common source allowed a new, more sophisticated level of analysis to be done, utilizing all of the analyst's estimates, not just a single estimate.

This ability to use large number of estimates by professional money managers in any formal way led to the creation of the earnings revision model. This model was the first structured use of expectational data. In fact, the earnings revision model was the first successful use of behavioral finance concepts in portfolio management (although at the time these models were created, behavioral finance did not exist as a field of study).

Analysts' estimate revisions explain price changes

The concept behind the earnings revision model is simple. If new information exists, it will be picked up by the analysts, and will eventually be incorporated into the price of the stock. As this information flows into the marketplace through the analysts, their earnings estimate revisions will form trends. These trends can be invested in and profits generated from doing so.

How and why does this work? To start with, a corporation's earnings are a major factor in determining the price of a stock. If markets are even reasonably efficient, past earnings are already reflected in the price of the stock. Efficient market theory suggests that even the expectation of future earnings is already in the price of a stock. If this is true, prices will follow changes in those expectations, as seen in Exhibit 11.1.

Since price and estimated earnings have a simultaneous relationship, what can you do to predict price? You need to be able to predict future estimate changes in order to predict future prices. In order to predict future changes, something has to be predictable about how analysts revise their forecasts. In fact, analyst's changes follow predictable trending patterns.

Exhibit 11.1

Stock prices follow earnings

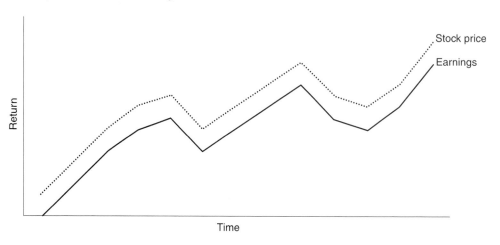

Source: Authors' own.

Analyst's estimates form trends

Let's take a hypothetical example to show how estimates form trends. Let's look at a situation where 10 analysts follow a stock. Every analyst is predicting earnings for the next fiscal year to be US$1.00. The analyst at one of the large brokerage firms puts the company's financial information into a spreadsheet, and models earnings. Next, the analyst reads news stories, interviews company management, and reads the unofficial web site about the company. The analyst comes away convinced that the company is being too conservative in their estimates for next year by 20 cents per share. What does the analyst do? Does the analyst raise his/her estimate by 20 cents? Absolutely not. The analyst raises his/her estimate by 5 cents per share to see what the other analysts will do.

Analysts now pay a lot of attention to each other. According to former FirstCall Director of Quantitative Research, Stan Levine, in 1997 FirstCall did a study of how fast it took analysts to react to a significant move by one analyst. The FirstCall study showed that, within 48 hours, virtually 100% of all analysts following a company had reacted to a significant move by a fellow analyst.

Why does the analyst only raise their estimate by a small amount? Many investment professionals speculate that it has to do with risk. Analyst positions for brokerage firms are in great demand, as they combine significant pay with enormous prestige. Anyone who works a lifetime to achieve one of these positions does not want to do anything to endanger their position. Therefore, analysts give indications of potential new information without wanting to commit to the magnitude of that information. Waiting to see how other analysts react allows an analyst to confirm their information, makes them more confident, and allows them to issue a new estimate, perhaps increasing another 5 cents. After the analyst has raised his/her estimate by 5 cents, if the other analysts follow then a trend starts to form. It is this trend that is the basis for all earnings revision models (see Exhibit 11.2).

Exhibit 11.2

Revisions rise in distinct steps

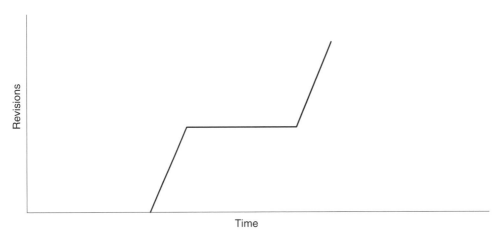

Source: Authors' own.

Earnings revision model

The way most investment professionals take advantage of these trends is by using an earnings revision model. The classic earnings revision model is constructed using three components: change in the mean, the diffusion index, and a leading/lagging indicator.

Exhibit 11.3 is the earnings summary page available from First Call of a prominent S&P 500 firm, which we will use as an example of how to calculate the earnings revision model.

Change in the mean

The first indication of a trend being formed in the analyst revisions is a change in the mean estimate. As an analyst revises upward or downward, that new estimate is included in the calculation of the new mean.

Let's look at 'Large Firm' to see the effect this has. 'Large Firm' has a current estimate at US$3.25 for the fiscal year ending 30 September 2002. Ten analysts follow the company. The range of estimates is US$3.00 to US$3.70. The analyst from 'Big Insurance Company' currently has an estimate of US$3.70, and has not revised it for the past 32 days. 'Big Insurance Company' analyst reviews the latest information from the company, the other analysts, and his own work, and concludes that US$3.30 is a better estimate. In this case, let's suppose the analyst revises downward from US$3.70 to US$3.30. That change will cause the mean to drop from US$3.25 to US$3.21. This is a drop of 1.23%.

Diffusion index

Once you have determined whether or not the mean has changed, you need to determine if it is part of a trend. The fact that the mean has changed does not mean that the change is due to a

87

Exhibit 11.3

Earnings summary page

Large S&P 500 firm	First Call Earnings Estimate Detail

Consensus summary

Year ending	Q1 Dec	Q2 Mar	Q3 Jun	Q4 Sep	FY Annual	Number of brokers	Cal year annual
2003	–	–	–	–	3.95	5	–
2002	0.74A	0.67	0.84	0.98	3.25	10	3.44
2001	0.57A	0.65A	0.72A	0.86A	2.80A	14	2.97A

Analyst detail (FYE Sep 2003)

Broker name	Q1 2-Dec	Q2 3-Mar	Q3 3-Jun	Q4 3-Sep	FY Annual	Last confirmed/ revised/orig.	
-30DayAgoMean:	0.83	0.91	1.13	1.23	3.97	–	15-Feb
Big bank.:	–	–	–	–	4.35	–	12-Mar
Previous:	–	–	–	–	4.45	–	16-Jan
Money center broker:	–	–	–	–	4	–	13-Mar
Previous:	–	–	–	–	4.45	–	6-Feb
Regional broker:	–	–	–	–	3.5	–	11-Mar
Previous:	–	–	–	–	3.85	–	14-Feb
Independent analyst:	–	–	–	–	4	–	4-Mar
Previous:	–	–	–	–	4.35	–	13-Feb
Big insurance company:	–	–	–	–	3.65	–	15-Feb
Previous:	–	–	–	–	4.15	–	14-Feb

First Call consensus statistics

	Q1	Q2	Q3	Q4	FY		
Number of brokers:	0	0	0	0	5	–	
Current mean:	–	–	–	–	3.95	18-Mar-02	
Previous mean:	–	–	–	–	3.97	4-Mar-02	
Standard deviation:	–	–	–	–	0.23		
Report date:	01/15w				–	–	

Analyst detail (FYE Sep 2002)

Broker name	Q1 1-Dec	Q2 2-Mar	Q3 2-Jun	Q4 2-Sep	FY Annual	Last confirmed/ revised/orig.	
-30DayAgoMean:	0.72	0.67	0.84	0.99	3.26	–	15-Feb
Big broker:	0.74A	0.65	0.85	0.96	3.2	–	12-Mar
Previous:	0.72	0.8	0.95	1.14	3.63	–	6-Feb
Bigger broker:	0.74A	0.69	0.76	0.91	3.1	–	21-Feb
Previous:	0.76	0.77	0.88	1.01	3.4	–	14-Feb
Money center bank:	0.74A	0.67	–	–	3.35	–	13-Mar
Previous:	0.72	0.77	–	–	3.45	–	7-Feb
Regional broker:	0.74A	0.67	0.75	0.85	3	–	11-Mar
Previous:	0.72	0.77	0.82	0.92	3.25	–	14-Feb
Independent analyst:	0.74A	0.69	0.9	1	3.33	–	4-Mar

Exhibit 11.3 *continued*

Earnings summary page

Previous:	0.72	0.82	1	1.12	3.68	–	13-Feb
Biggest broker:	0.74A	0.68	0.82	1	2.24		
Previous:	0.72	0.77	0.82	1	3.25		-Mar
Big insurance company:	0.74A	0.87	0.95	1.15	3.70	–	15-Feb
Previous:	0.72	0.87	0.95	1.19	3.75	–	14-Feb
Bigger insurance company:	0.74A	0.67	0.82	1.07	3.3	–	Mar-Mar
Previous:	0.72	0.82	0.95	1.19	3.7	–	14-Feb
Independent analyst:	0.74A	0.69	0.9	1	3.33	–	4-Mar
Previous:	0.72	0.82	1	1.12	3.68	–	13-Feb
Independent analyst:	0.74A	0.69	0.9	1	3.33	–	4-Mar
Previous:	0.72	0.82	1	1.12	3.68	–	13-Feb
Biggest insurance company:	0.74A	0.67	0.82	1.07	3.3	–	15-Feb
Previous:	0.72	0.82	0.95	1.19	3.7	–	14-Feb

First Call consensus statistics

Number of brokers:	10	10	10	10	10	–	
Current mean:	0.74A	0.67	0.84	0.98	3.25	18-Mar-02	
Previous mean:	0.73	0.68	0.86	0.99	3.26	25-Feb-02	
Standard deviation:	0.01	0.01	0.05	0.06	0.1		
Report date:	01/15A	25-Apr	07/18w	10/18w	–	–	

Source: First Call.

trend. Do not forget that only a trend signifies new information coming into the marketplace. That new information is what will drive prices. If three analysts revise upward by 10 cents each, and three analysts revise downward 5 cents each, the mean will rise. However, three analysts revising each direction does not signal that new information has come into the marketplace. If five of the six or more had been revising upward, then it is clearer that they are all reacting to something. That something can be a news item about the company, a company press release, or another analyst, but there is a clear reaction taking place. Therefore, we are looking for more analysts moving in one direction, and that is what the diffusion index will show us.

This component of the earnings revision model is the easiest to calculate. It is the number of upward revisions minus the number of downward revisions divided by the total of the upward revisions plus the downward revision:

$$\text{Diffusion index} = (\text{Upward revisions} - \text{Downward revisions}) / (\text{Ups} + \text{Downs})$$

The reason that it is divided by ups plus downs, instead of total number of estimates, is that if only five of 10 analysts following a company are making timely revisions, then the 'diffusion index' can create a false signal. If three of the five active analysts make upward revisions, a trend is forming, but the 'diffusion index' will be (3 – 0/10) or 0.3 instead of (3 – 0)/(3 + 0) or 1.0. The latter is a much stronger signal and is providing the proper indication of a trend former. The former is a much weaker signal. The same signal would come from six analysts revising upward and three downward ((6 – 3)/10) which is a weaker trend then all of the analysts revising upward.

Timing is another issue. How do you cut off what revisions to look at? In the 1980s, portfolio managers would look at the most recent revision by all of the analysts following a stock, and that worked for a few years. A refinement was made when managers started to look only at the most recent estimates. Let's look at our 'Large Firm' example. During the last 30 days, 'Large Firm' has had zero ups and two downs for a diffusion index of -1.0 $((0 - 2)/(0 + 2))$. Most people currently use a fixed number of days to cut off how old the estimates can be. It is felt that beyond 30 days is information that is already priced into the stock.

A more sophisticated analysis is cluster analysis. Cluster analysis utilizes a number of factors in determining the latest group of earnings estimates. It is a way to determine when new information is flowing into the marketplace about a stock. Cluster analysis allows the flexibility that a fixed cut-off date does not. A cluster could occur in the past few days or the past few weeks. When calculating diffusion or any of the other revision model sections, it suggests the best data to include in that calculation.

Leading/lagging indicator

So you have determined a trend, but are you early or late? Now that a trend is occurring, it is imperative to be early in the trend and not late. If 10 analysts all react to a piece of information, by the time the last analyst reacts the information should be reasonably reflected in the price. When the first analyst uncovers new information, they change their estimate. This action causes other analysts to follow in reaction to the news. Usually, the first analysts react very quickly to estimate changes by other analysts. These analysts tend to be from leading brokerage firms with significant resources. Smaller firms generally have a harder time covering the universe of stocks on a timely basis. It may take an analyst who covers twice as many stocks longer to react to new information. This analyst may wait several weeks before responding, and may be the eighth of 10 analysts covering a company to respond. By the time this analyst reacts, the price has already reacted, and the ability to predict future price changes is lost.

So how do you ensure that you are leading the trend and not lagging it? By seeing if the move is toward or away from the mean estimate, and how far away it is. First, calculate the standard deviation of the estimates. This will allow you to compare the significance of the move across securities. Next, calculate how far the move is in terms of standard deviations (the z-score). A move away from the mean is positive for moving above the mean and negative for moving below.

How do you take the above information, calculate an earnings revision score for many companies, and determine which one is better?

The variables need to be combined in an optimal way to create a final score. A common method is to analyze the distribution and calculate a z-score for each item. For this example, the five observations were equalized to force a range of $+2$ to -2 for each variable before combining. Another concern is the determination of weights for each part. A typical decision rule would suggest, when lacking superior information about the value of each variable, equal weighting is best. Others take a regressional approach to the problem. Scores are calculated going back in time. A regression analysis is completed that shows the predictive ability of each component. The components are then weighted based on the predicted contribution. During the early 1990s, when this type of analysis was done, many firms came to the conclusion that the largest weight should go to the diffusion index. Today, based on advances in calculating the leading/lagging indicator, this is no longer the norm. Another alternative is ordinal weighting, which we will show at the bottom of this analysis.

Here is an example of five companies:

Company 1
Number of analysts following the firm: 10
Mean of the estimates after most recent revision: US$3.43
Mean of estimates before most recent revision: US$3.40
Most recent revision: US$3.60 (from US$3.30)
Standard deviation of the estimates: 0.20
Number of revisions up in last 30 days: 8
Number of revisions down in last 30 days: 1

Change in the mean: US$3.43 – US$3.40/US$3.40 = 1.5%
Diffusion: (8 – 1)/(8 + 1) = 78%
Leading/lagging: US$3.60 – 3.40/0.20 = 1.0

Revision score (after adjusting the above date for distributional properties): 1.35

Company 2
Number of analysts following the firm: 10
Mean of the estimates after most recent revision: US$1.20
Mean of estimates before most recent revision: US$1.22
Most recent revision: US$1.40 (from US$1.20)
Standard deviation of the estimates: 0.10
Number of revisions up in last 30 days: 3
Number of revisions down in last 30 days: 2

Change in the mean: US$1.22 – US$1.20/ US$1.20 = 2.0%
Diffusion: (3 – 2)/(3 + 2) = 20%
Leading/lagging: US$1.40 – 1.20/0.10 = 2.0

Revision score (after adjusting the above date for distributional properties): 1.47

Company 3
Number of analysts following the firm: 5
Mean of the estimates after most recent revision: US$2.03
Mean of estimates before most recent revision: US$2.00
Most recent revision: US$2.25 (from US$1.95)
Standard deviation of the estimates: 0.17
Number of revisions up in last 30 days: 2
Number of revisions down in last 30 days: 0

Change in the mean: US$2.03 – US$2.00/ US$2.00 = 1.76%
Diffusion: (2 – 0)/(2 + 0) = 100%
Leading/lagging: US$2.25 – 2.00/0.17 = 1.47

Revision score (after adjusting the above date for distributional properties): 1.75

Company 4
Number of analysts following the firm: 15
Mean of the estimates after most recent revision: US$3.09
Mean of estimates before most recent revision: US$3.12
Most recent revision: US$3.11 (from US$3.45)
Standard deviation of the estimates: 0.27
Number of revisions up in last 30 days: 5
Number of revisions down in last 30 days: 6

Change in the mean: US$3.09 – US$3.12/ US$3.12 = –1.26%
Diffusion: (5 – 6)/(5 + 6) = –9%
Leading/lagging: US$3.11 – 3.12/0.27 = –0.04

Revision score (after adjusting the above date for distributional properties): -0.49

Company 5
Number of analysts following the firm: 10
Mean of the estimates after most recent revision: US$2.29
Mean of estimates before most recent revision: US$2.26
Most recent revision: US$2.55 (from US$2.25)
Standard deviation of the estimates: 0.30
Number of revisions up in last 30 days: 5
Number of revisions down in last 30 days: 2

Change in the mean: US$2.29 – US$2.26/ US$2.26 = 1.0%
Diffusion: (5 – 2)/(5 + 2) = 43%
Leading/lagging: US$2.55 – 2.26/0.30 = 0.97

Revision score (after adjusting the above date for distributional properties): 0.94

In the final analysis, Company 3 is the best company to invest in, based purely on earnings revision scores. Its mean is rising as both of the recent estimates have been up. The most recent estimate was 25 cents above the previous mean. All three components of the revision score were positive. It had the best diffusion index, and was second in the leading/lagging indicator and second in change in the mean. That led to a combined score greater than any other company.

If we had chosen another weighting scheme, ordinal weighting, the calculation would have been as follows:

Company 1
Change in the mean rank: 3
Diffusion rank: 2
Leading/lagging rank: 3
Overall rank: 8/3 = 2.67

Company 2
Change in the mean rank: 1
Diffusion rank: 4
Leading/lagging rank: 1
Overall rank: 6/3 = 2.0

Company 3
Change in the mean rank: 2
Diffusion rank: 1
Leading/lagging rank: 2
Overall rank: 5/3 = 1.67

Company 4
Change in the mean rank: 5
Diffusion rank: 5
Leading/lagging rank: 5
Overall rank: 15/3 = 5

Company 5
Change in the mean rank: 4
Diffusion rank: 3
Leading/lagging rank: 4
Overall rank: 11/3 = 3.67

How did our two different combinations compare? If we were trying to create a model with an equal balance between the factors, we did well either way.

	Z-score rank	Ordinal rank
Company 1	3	3
Company 2	2	2
Company 3	1	1
Company 4	5	5
Company 5	4	4

Combining data is not an exact science. Looking at multiple combinations and stress testing the power of each will go a long way in showing you whether your model is really finding good underlying information or is simply combined in a way that works well with a particular data set.

Will analyst revisions continue to work?

This question has been asked throughout the 1990s, and the answer has always been proven to be yes. Exhibit 11.4 shows that analyst revisions have not been successful over the past two years. There could be many reasons for this poor performance, many focusing on a change in the long-term effectiveness of the concept. Some ideas from Morgan Stanley (2001) are listed below:

1. *Bear market.* Since the most recent years are a bear market, they may support a theory that revision models do not work in bear markets. This is not borne out by historical tests, which show that revision strategies have worked in both bull and bear markets.
2. *Too many players.* If too many people execute a strategy, common sense suggests that the effect will be arbitraged away. In this case, people have used revision strategies for years,

Exhibit 11.4

Impact of revision forecasts

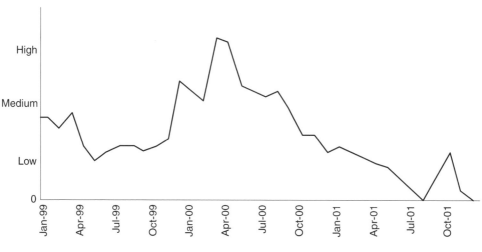

Source: Authors' own.

and the effect has withstood the increase. In those cases, the argument has been made that everyone calculates revisions differently and at different times, so there is no universal signal to trigger buying or selling.

3. *Regulation FD.* Reg FD might make information going from the companies to the analysts more uniform, but it does not affect the way that analysts create estimates or the psychology of analyst behavior, so it is unlikely that this change has any effect.

4. *Value is now in favor.* Just as with the bear market concept, historical tests have shown that revision strategies work in both value and growth driven markets.

5. *Recent focus on earnings.* With so many players focusing on earnings and with a spate of negative news, analysts would need to process information differently for this to be a factor. Once again, this is unlikely.

Morgan Stanley feels that the best explanation for recent poor revision returns is that:

> An analyst growth bias in a terrible growth market combined with the inherent difficulty of forecasting earnings as they crash is the most plausible explanation. If this is right, we would expect that revisions may begin to work again after earnings stabilize and analysts adjust to the new environment.

Summary

Earnings revisions models are a tool that can and should be used by every investor. As has been shown in Chapter 3, 'The role of analysts', in absolute terms, analysts are wrong by an average of 41%. Properly understanding how analysts revise estimates and what information you can glean from that process is a necessary skill.

Further reading

The classic paper on this topic was written by Lang Wheeler and included in Brian's earlier book *The Handbook of Corporate Earnings Analysis*.

Wheeler, L. (1994), 'Changes in Consensus Earnings Estimates and Their Impact on Stock Returns', Brian R. Bruce and C. Epstein (eds), *The Handbook of Corporate Earnings Analysis*, Chicago, Probus.

Morgan Stanley's recent study is:

'Whither Analysts Revisions?' (2001), Global Equity and Derivative Markets Quantitative Strategies, December.

Other useful papers include:

DeBondt, W., and Forbes, W. (1999), 'Herding in Analyst Earnings Forecasts: Evidence from the United Kingdom', *European Financial Management,* Vol. 5, No. 2.

DeBondt, W., and Thaler, R. (1990), 'Do Security Analysts Overreact?', *AEA Papers and Proceedings,* May.

Jha, V., and Mozes, H. (2001), 'Forecasting Changes in Consensus Earnings Estimates', Working Paper, April.

Chapter 12

Earnings surprise

Things almost always turn out otherwise than one anticipates.

Maurice Hulst

What is earnings surprise? It is an earnings report that differs from what analysts were expecting. Earnings surprise often causes a substantial movement in the stock's price. This description can now be found on many financial websites. It shows how common the idea of earnings surprise has become. In the 1960s, the concept of earnings surprise was limited to a few academics doing research on an effect that was not known to many sophisticated investors.

History

The relationship between corporate earnings information and stock prices has been an active area of financial research since the 1960s. The origins of this research can be traced to the notion of stock market efficiency, which implies that all publicly available information should rapidly get reflected in stock prices in an unbiased manner. Due to this, security prices should quickly react to earnings numbers when they are released. The magnitude and direction of the market reaction should be related to the degree to which the information contained in earnings disclosures is new (unexpected). In an early study on this effect, Ball and Brown (1968) were able to document a significant pre-earnings announcement drift in the stock prices of the companies in their sample. Exhibit 12.1 shows that for two measures of unexpected earnings (variable 1: net income and variable 2: EPS), this drift was positive for companies that reported higher earnings than expected (an excess return of about 7% over the 12 months preceding the announcement), and negative for companies whose earnings came in below expectations (an approximate –9.5% excess return over the same period).[1] Furthermore, companies that had the largest earnings deviations from the prior year (the biggest surprises) experienced the greatest reaction.

Two features of Exhibit 12.1 deserve further comment. First, consistent with the thesis of informational efficiency of the stock market, Ball and Brown found that about 85–90% of the market reaction to earnings announcements occurred in the months preceding the announcement and only 10–15% during the announcement month itself. This is consistent with the existence of analysts whose forecasts and forecast revisions cause prices to continuously move up (down) during the year, in accord with favorable (unfavorable) news. Subsequent studies obtained even stronger results. Brown, Griffin, Hagerman, and Zmijewski (1987) attributed this improvement to the fact that analysts' forecasts are better predictors of actual earnings than mechanical forecasts of the type used by Ball and Brown, because they are likely to incorporate the more timely and broader sources of information typically available to market participants. Their work led to the widespread use of analysts' forecasts as proxies for market expectations. The availability of large historical databases of analysts' forecasts in electronic form and readily accessible online

Exhibit 12.1

Pre-announcement drift

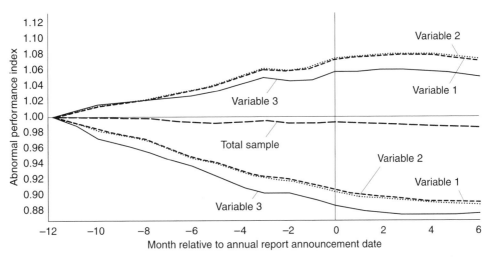

Source: Ball and Brown (1968).

updates to such data served to further popularize the use of analysts' forecasts in investment research and practice.

The second noteworthy aspect of Exhibit 12.1 is that the market reaction to positive and negative earnings surprises is not symmetric. Firms whose reported earnings fall below expectations appear to experience a larger negative reaction before, during, and after the month of the earnings announcement than those that surprise on the upside.

Finally, as Exhibit 12.1 indicates, excess returns associated with extreme earnings surprises seemed to persist for several months after the earnings report. This implies that abnormal returns could be earned by forming portfolios based on the sign and magnitude of earnings surprises. This observation led to the use of standardized unexpected earnings (SUE) scores in stock valuation. SUE scores are discussed in the next section in context of our discussion of earnings surprise measurement.

Measurement issues

As mentioned above, one key component in measuring the earnings surprise for a company is the analyst's forecast of earnings for the company. Unless the company is very small, it is likely to be covered by more than one analyst, and earnings forecasts issued by different analysts for the same company and fiscal period may differ. A conventional approach to incorporating the divergent views of multiple analysts is to construct a consensus forecast, such as a mean (or median) of all currently available forecasts. If one believes that each individual analyst's forecast of earnings measures the company's actual earnings with some error, but that these errors are idiosyncratic across analysts, this approach has the merit of reducing the error ('noise') inherent in the individual forecasts.

Stock returns from an earnings surprise strategy depend on variation in the magnitude and direction of the surprises. The magnitude of the surprise cannot be measured in purely monetary terms, since the impact of an actual earnings report of 10 cents a share by a company for which the mean analyst expectation was 5 cents (a 100% surprise) is likely to be much greater than the case where the analysts' forecast was US$1.00 and the company reported actual earnings of US$1.05 per share (a 5% surprise). Note that in both cases, the actual reported earnings beat expectations by the same amount (5 cents per share). The example illustrates the need to account for differences in scale when studying the relation between earnings surprises and stock prices.

The earnings surprise number can be normalized by a variety of deflators, such as the actual or forecast earnings, as indicated in the above example. One problem with these approaches is that they tend to break down when the actual (or forecast) earnings are negative. An alternative is to use the absolute value of the actual or forecast earnings instead. Even so, difficulties can arise in cases where the earnings number used for scaling is very small. Deflators close to zero magnify the actual surprise, leading to large cross sectional variations that are unrelated to significant differences between expectations and the actual outcomes. In such cases, the stock price at the time of the forecast is often used as a deflator.

The above discussion has focused on operational factors that can affect the robustness of earnings surprise measures. However, when constructing such measures, it is equally important to consider the reliability of the consensus earnings forecasts. The market reacts to a company's earnings announcement because it triggers a revision of beliefs about the company's future (for example, its ability to grow or pay a certain stream of dividends). The extent of this revision depends on the strength (consistency) of investors' pre-announcement views about a particular earnings outcome. If the market is fairly certain about what the earnings for a company are likely to be, an earnings announcement that deviates from that expectation constitutes unambiguously good (or bad) news, and the resulting price reaction is likely to be sharp and swift. On the other hand, if there is considerable uncertainty about the earnings outcome, the announcement of earnings primarily serves to dispel uncertainty about future outcomes. A widely accepted measure of earnings surprise that incorporates this notion is the standardized unexpected earnings or SUE score proposed by Latane and Jones (1977). The SUE score is the difference between the actual earnings and expected earnings deflated by a measure of uncertainty in the earnings forecast. To calculate a stock's SUE, three items of data are needed: the company's latest reported earnings, the last consensus earnings estimate before the release of the actual earnings, and the standard deviation of the individual analysts' forecasts that make up the consensus. The SUE can then be calculated as:

$$\frac{\text{Actual earnings} - \text{Consensus earnings forecast}}{\text{Standard deviation of analysts' forecasts}}$$

The more extreme the value of the resulting number, the more likely it is that the company's earnings announcement will have a significant effect on its share price. The intuition underlying the SUE score follows from our earlier observation that the market reaction to the surprise associated with an earnings announcement depends not only on the magnitude of the surprise (captured in the numerator of the calculation), but also on the uncertainty inherent in the forecast of expected earnings. The denominator of the SUE score captures this uncertainty by directly gauging the extent to which analysts disagree about the earnings outcome for a company.[2] However, as with other earnings surprise measures, caution needs to be exercised in the computation of SUE scores in cases where sufficient data is not available for computation. For small companies, the number of analysts following the company may be small (often one or two), making it difficult or impossible to compute the standard deviation of forecasts.

Clearly, the benefits of using any particular deflator are debatable, and much depends on one's view of what drives the stock price reaction to earnings surprises and the nature of the data available. If the time series process underlying earnings is considered stable, focusing on large percentage changes will capture the stock market effects of unusual earnings events. On the other hand, price deflation is appealing since it directly associates earnings changes with the valuation impact of those changes. SUE scores are intuitively pleasing because they allow us to incorporate not only the effect of extraordinary earnings reports, but also the characteristics of the forecasts themselves into the surprise metric in a logical fashion. This reason and the fact that SUE was the first published indicator of surprise have made the SUE scores the most commonly used measure of earnings surprise.

Earning abnormal returns from earnings surprises

In our discussion of the Ball and Brown (1968) study, we alluded briefly to the nature of the market reaction to earnings surprises around the time of the earnings announcement. In a pattern confirmed by several independent academic studies, Exhibit 12.1 indicated that stocks with the largest positive (negative) surprises move higher (lower) before the earnings announcement, jump (drop) dramatically during the report week, and then continue to drift up (down) during subsequent weeks. The pattern of market reaction to earnings surprises during and before the announcement month confirms our intuition that, as the uncertainty about future earnings is gradually resolved during the year, the good or bad news should manifest itself in stock prices via continual revisions of forecasts by analysts, interim corporate disclosures, and leakage of information into the market through the information search activities of other market participants. However, the post-announcement reaction is counter-intuitive, in that after earnings have been publicly announced, the information in the earnings release should be rapidly incorporated into market prices in an unbiased fashion, rather than continuing to drift up or down over a prolonged period. In the early 1970s, some researchers examined this post-announcement drift in greater detail, noting that it was contrary to the notion of market efficiency. The post announcement drift persisted well into the 1990s, and was subjected to rigorous academic research because it contradicted the notion of market efficiency. The anomaly could not be explained even after controlling for risk, size, and a variety of other factors that could affect stock returns, and with investors eyeing potential short-term gains from trading on earnings surprises, SUE scores soon became a standard component of stock valuation models. SUE scores performed well from 1987 to 1998, displaying correlations of as much as 30% with one-month ahead stock returns and predicting the direction of subsequent stock price movements correctly over 83% of the time. Results for longer holding periods (two or three months) were similar, and enabled investors to earn excess returns of 4–5%.[3] However, of late the ability of SUE scores to forecast one-month ahead returns has begun to diminish. For example, in 1999, the correlation between the two was negative for six out of 12 months. To a large extent, this should have been expected, for discovery of information inevitably leads to its reflection in market prices. Indeed, what was surprising was the fact that the effect per-

Exhibit 12.2

Earnings expectation life cycle

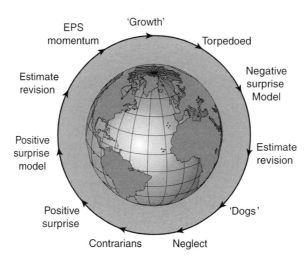

'Growth'

EPS momentum

Torpedoed

Estimate revision

Negative surprise Model

Positive surprise model

Estimate revision

Positive surprise

'Dogs'

Contrarians   Neglect

Source: Merrill Lynch.

sisted for so long after its discovery and exploitation. However, two additional factors have contributed to the decline in the effectiveness of SUE scores: (1) the corruption of consensus estimates as a measure of market expectations over this period, and (2) the manipulation of reported earnings by corporate management, subjects to which we shall return at the end of this chapter.

As the ability of SUE scores to predict future stock price movements has diminished, and the reaction times to earnings announcements have shrunk, opportunities to profit from earnings surprises at or after the earnings announcement date have become scarce. In turn, these developments have spurred efforts to capture pre-announcement returns as a means of benefiting from earnings surprise events. In order to do so, it is necessary to predict earnings surprises. The logic underlying earnings surprise prediction models comes from the post-earnings announcement drift in stock prices discussed earlier. Bernard and Thomas (1990) suggested that this drift occurs because 'stock prices fail to fully reflect the implications of current earnings for future earnings.' Using quarterly data, they found a positive correlation between the current period's earnings surprise and excess return after the following three consecutive earnings announcements, and a negative correlation with the post-announcement return four quarters ahead in the future. This pattern appears to reflect a similar correlation among consecutive earnings surprises, and forms the basis of the 'earnings expectations life cycle' proposed by Richard Bernstein (see Exhibit 12.2).[4]

The earnings expectations life cycle is suggestive of incomplete adjustments to earnings expectations by analysts. It implies that the market fails to fully recognize that earnings surprises repeat in the same direction, and this favorable (unfavorable) earnings news is gradually incorporated into stock prices over subsequent quarters, causing upward (downward) post-announcement drift. The market underestimates the magnitude (but not the direction) of the serial correlation. Building on these insights, Brown, Han, Keon, and Quinn (1996), among others, have constructed surprise prediction models that exploit the serial correlation

Exhibit 12.3

SUE quintiles 1–5: cumulative returns around report date, 1992–96

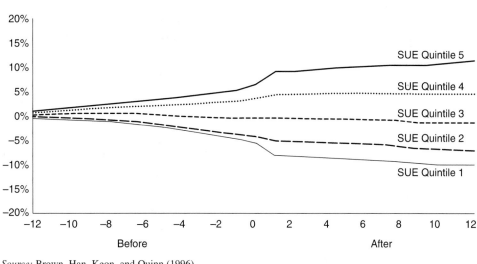

Source: Brown, Han, Keon, and Quinn (1996).

of earnings surprises. As Exhibit 12.3 indicates, use of such models to predict earnings surprises can produce an excess stock return performance of 8–9% over the three-month period preceding the earnings announcement.

A natural question that arises at this juncture is whether surprise prediction models will lose importance as a factor in stock valuation models over time, as their use also becomes widespread and the ability to earn excess returns from them dissipates. We believe that may not be the case, for two reasons. First, unlike SUE scores, earnings surprise predictors do not rely on publicly available information in order to work, that is, the trading rule is proprietary and its efficacy depends on the quality of the surprise predictor. Second, one of the primary factors that led to the demise of SUE scores (manipulation of consensus earnings forecasts by managers seeking to meet or beat market expectations) does not affect pre-announcement returns. Indeed, there is evidence to suggest that adjustment of earnings forecasts by analysts in the pre-announcement period (based on management 'guidance') is not only helpful in building surprise prediction models, but also drives the drift in stock prices during the pre-announcement period. However, recent changes in the regulations that govern financial analysts' disclosures may limit the value of this signal in the years to come. Following allegations that (a) companies selectively disclose information to favored analysts, and (b) brokerage houses that employ these analysts tend to inform their largest (most lucrative) clients of upcoming rating changes before the analysts' research reports are officially released, the SEC has issued Regulation FD to protect smaller investors. In the wake of Regulation FD, companies have also become sensitive to the possibility of litigation. Amid a proliferation of shareholder class action lawsuits alleging that investment losses were caused because the guidance provided to investors was too optimistic, they have tended towards providing less forward looking information. These changes are likely to reduce the information leakage that drives the upward (downward) drift in stock prices prior to a favorable (unfavorable) earnings announcement.

Factors affecting the strength of the earnings surprise-stock return relationship

The relationship between SUE scores and stock returns at and after the earnings announcement depends not only on the magnitude and direction of the reported surprise but also on the characteristics of the reporting companies. Companies with low P/E multiples (value stocks) tend to show greater reaction on the upside when the earnings surprise is positive, while those with high P/E ratios (growth stocks) experience greater negative fallout from an earnings report that disappoints. The reasons for this phenomenon may be traced back to the earnings expectations life cycle discussed earlier. Recall that in the late part of the cycle, as the estimate revisions for positive surprise stocks turn positive, momentum investors pile into these stocks, causing their P/E ratios to go up. When expectations rise to unrealistic levels, subsequent negative surprises 'torpedo' these very same growth stocks, causing them to 'sink' rapidly at the time of the earnings announcement. David Dreman[5] suggests that the above relationship between P/E ratios and market reaction to earnings surprises can be used to earn abnormal returns, as depicted in Exhibit 12.4.

Another factor that affects this relationship is firm size. Bhushan (1989) has shown that smaller firms tend to have fewer analysts following their stock. If analysts are viewed as information intermediaries whose forecasting activities serve to incorporate value-relevant information into market prices, one would expect smaller firm size (lower analyst following) to be associated with larger earnings surprises. This is because in the case of a smaller company, less information is likely to have been impounded into its stock price prior to its earnings announcement. The quantity and quality of pre-disclosure information increase, earnings surprises, and the market's reaction to them are smaller. They also report that the speed of stock prices adjustment following earnings surprises is greater when the quality and

Exhibit 12.4

Factors affecting the strength of the earning surprise – stock return relationship

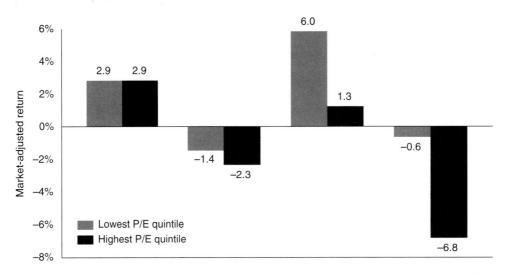

Source: David Dreman.

quantity of analysts' forecasts is high. There is an inverse relationship between the degree of prominence of a firm (as measured by the amount of coverage it receives in the financial press) and the market reaction to its earnings announcements. However, firm size can proxy for a variety of factors, such as risk, so any conclusions should be drawn with caution. For example, the level of institutional shareholding in a firm has been shown to vary directly with firm size.

Other characteristics of the firm and its information environment influence the market reaction to earnings surprises in a similar manner. For example, poor earnings predictability is also expected to be associated with a bigger market reaction to earnings. Pre-disclosure information asymmetry (uncertainty about future earnings) and firm size have a close inverse relationship, due to the same underlying reason: if fewer analysts expend effort in discovering and disseminating information about smaller companies, investors will have less knowledge (greater uncertainty) about future earnings of small companies, and therefore the market reaction to their earnings announcements should be more pronounced. This uncertainty is further enhanced by the fact that the earnings stream of a small company is inherently more variable, and thus more difficult to predict. Building on these insights, several researchers have examined the relationship between earnings predictability[6] and the market reaction to earnings announcements. The relationship between earnings predictability and stock price reaction to earnings announcements is somewhat complex, and is related to analysts' incentives. Sell-side analysts face a multitude of conflicting incentives when formulating their forecasts. Since they work for brokerage, firms their forecasts tend to have an optimistic bias, because a rosy forecast for a company can be used to induce both current as well as potential stockholders to buy that company's stock.[7] This generates trading commissions for the brokerage firms that employ the analysts. Further, analysts rely on corporate management as a primary source of information. Optimistic forecasts improve their relationships with company management, thereby enhancing their access to corporate information. The incentive for analysts to acquire information, and consequently such biases, are greater in the case of companies whose earnings are difficult to predict. At the same time, however, most analysts are averse to taking the risk of making bold forecasts away from the prevailing consensus, for fear of damaging their reputations. As a result, they exhibit 'herding' behavior, that is, they tend to revise their published estimates toward the consensus. These tendencies have two observable effects. First, the dispersion (standard deviation) of their forecasts is reduced. Second, since analysts are reluctant to revise their forecasts downwards, it increases the mean of the forecasts. As a result, SUE scores (especially negative SUE scores) become magnified, and larger price reactions occur when earnings are announced. Again, herding behavior is greater in cases where earnings are difficult to predict, because the risk of being wrong on a bold forecast that deviates from the consensus is higher.

Latane and Jones (1977) found that excess returns associated with large SUE scores are systematically different in up and down markets. In particular, they discovered that high positive SUE scores were followed by lower returns when the market was rising, and higher returns when the market was falling. Moreover, high negative SUE scores were associated with a smaller negative return when the market was falling, and a higher negative return when the market was rising. These findings are open to a variety of interpretations. If what really matters to investors is relative (rather than absolute) performance, one could argue that from an investment point of view, companies whose earnings beat expectations are relatively rare (and hence more desirable) in a down market, because they signal unusual ability to withstand the effect of poor economic conditions. Conversely, when the market is rising, an inability to meet expectations is more severely penalized, because the beneficial effects of general economic prosperity likely provide a boost to all but the most poor quality firms. A more subtle explanation for this result arises from the herding behavior discussed previously. Recall that analysts tend to revise their individual estimates upwards when they are below the consensus, but shy away from downward revisions if their last estimate is already above the prevailing consensus. This behavior is likely to reinforce the optimistic bias in analysts' forecast in up markets. Analysts tend to herd more in up markets than in down markets. Since herding behavior leads to poor information aggregation (that is, results in less independent information being made available to the market), 'news' tends to have a greater impact. This fact, taken together with our previous comment about greater optimistic bias in up markets, sets the stage for large negative surprises and accompanying large negative returns when markets are rising.

It also seems reasonable to expect that the market reaction to earnings surprises should vary by industry. One reason for this is that earnings predictability varies across industries, being particularly poor in cases such as information technology, where the environment changes quickly. In this context, it is important to note that the pattern of earnings predictability for a given industry can also change significantly over time. Prime examples are the telecommunications and utility industries, which have transitioned from being dominated by a few monopolies to a fiercely competitive landscape as a result of deregulation. Earnings predictability can also vary across industries according to the extent of management's ability to manipulate accruals (and hence reported earnings). In general, long-term accruals, such as depreciation, are less susceptible to such influences than current accruals, such as inventories and receivables, so that industry differences in this area can be expected to influence how the market reacts to earnings surprises. A second factor that can affect the impact of an earnings announcement is the nature of the disclosure environment. Analysts' earnings forecasts compete with other sources of information about companies in the stock market. To the extent information from alternative sources allows investors to construct reliable estimates of earnings, analysts' forecasts, and thereby the earnings surprises associated with them, may not matter a great deal. For instance, the stock prices of companies in the extractive industries appear to be driven in large part by macroeconomic factors, such as the demand for and supply of oil, which in turn may depend on extraneous events such as OPEC meetings, the political situation in the Middle East, or discovery of new natural gas reserves; in such cases, the information search activities of analysts may have relatively little impact. A final reason for cross-industry variation in market reactions to earnings surprises is the difference in analyst coverage, task complexity, and experience of analysts.

Finally, forecast horizons are important in considering the effect of earnings surprises on stock prices. Based on the general tendency of firms to delay the announcement of bad news, it is likely that for forecasts made toward the end of the fiscal year, the market has had more time to price good news, but bad news may not be fully incorporated into prices. This observation, in conjunction with the various restrictions on short sales mentioned earlier, has two implications. First, it may be easier to benefit from negative as opposed to positive earnings surprises, depending on the average age of the forecasts in the consensus. Second, since the P/E ratios of companies that announce good news climb as one approaches the end of the fiscal year, the spread between high and low P/E stocks should increase as the forecast horizon becomes shorter.

Ancillary relationships

Our discussion thus far has focused on the relationship between earnings surprises and stock prices. In addition to their impact on stock prices, earnings surprises also affect trading volume around earnings announcements. Pioneering work in this area found, not surprisingly, that the magnitude and duration of trading volume reaction to earnings announcements are increasing functions of the magnitude of the earnings surprise. In addition, evidence of an inverse relationship between trading volume and firm size can be attributed to differences in the availability of pre-disclosure information about small and large firms. The direction of the size effect is consistent with our previous discussion about the relationship between firm size and stock price reaction to earnings surprises.

A few researchers have also examined if a link exists between earnings surprises and bond prices. The argument that supports such a link is somewhat indirect; it is based on the view that stockholders and bondholders have a joint stake in a firm, and that the default risk on bonds is lower for firms that can maintain a continuous stream of high earnings. In the context of the discussion of earnings surprise prediction, we mentioned that earnings surprises are positively serially correlated. Thus, a positive earnings surprise, especially the first one in a series to come, signals to the market the ability of a firm to meet its contractual obligations of interest and principal payments to its bondholders. Indeed, many bond indenture agreements specify targets on earnings-based financial ratios, such as interest coverage. Failure to meet such targets can put the firm into technical default and force it to renegotiate bond agreements with its creditors, usually on less favorable terms.

An interesting relationship also exists between earnings surprises of a firm and the stock price behavior of other firms in the same or related industries. To the extent that common factors drive earnings outcomes for firms in the same industry, intuition suggests that a stock price reaction should occur for non-announcing firms as well. Han and Wild (1990), and Ramnath (2000), provide evidence of positive correlation between the stock price reaction of announcing and non-announcing firms in the same industry, and, by extrapolation, a relationship to the announcing firm's reported earnings surprise.[8] As can be expected, however, these (second-order) effects are smaller, though statistically significant. In this context, the impact of industry-specific information on stock prices of firms within that industry is of greater interest from an investment point of view.

Pitfalls in relying on the earnings surprise–stock price relationship

The preceding discussion has alluded briefly to the recent decline in the strength of the earnings–stock price relationship. Hence, over-reliance on naïve earnings surprise strategies can lead to disappointing investment performance unless these influences are taken into account. In this section, some possible reasons for this trend are explored. One cause is the gradual degradation in the quality of earnings forecasts. In our discussion of measurement issues, we mentioned the tradeoff between consensus and individual forecasts in forming the expectations from which earnings surprises are measured. Consensus forecasts offer the benefit of filtering out the biases inherent in individual analysts' forecasts. These optimistic biases arise due to analysts' incentives to gain access to (and thereby private information from) the management of the company for which forecasts are issued, or to build or maintain an investment banking relationship with that company (see for example, Dugar and Nathan (1995)).

However, this advantage comes at a cost: some forecasts comprising the consensus may be rather dated, as a result of which the effect of more recent (and presumably more valuable) information is diluted in the averaging process. A tradeoff may exist between recency and aggregation. Brown (1991) compared the predictive accuracy of (a) the most recent forecast, (b) the average of the three most recent forecasts, and (c) the average of the forecasts made in the past 30 days, and found the 30 day average to be the most accurate composite, though results varied by firm size. Several other factors, such as the analyst's expertise, characteristics of the brokerage firm employing the analyst, and the analyst's task complexity (measured by the number of companies and industries followed by the analyst), influence forecast accuracy. While such factors marginally improved the quality of consensus forecasts, forecast age had by far the greatest impact. On the other hand, the fact that the most recent, or even the average, of the three most recent forecasts does not perform as well indicates that using individual analysts' forecasts selected solely on the basis of forecast age is sub-optimal, because individual forecasts are prone to large errors or biases.

Mozes and Williams (1999) show that forming consensus forecasts based on 'clusters' of revisions (near-contemporaneous revisions by groups of analysts during a relatively recent time window) appears to optimize the tradeoff between the error in individual forecasts and the lack of timeliness that afflicts naïve aggregates, such as the mean of all available forecasts. Their argument is based on the premise that analysts typically revise their forecasts when significant new information about a company becomes available. Thus, a cluster of revisions signals the arrival of additional value-relevant information, whereas scattered revisions, while affecting the consensus, may merely be the result of an individual analyst falling in line with the prevailing views in the market. The quality of this consensus can be further improved by giving due weight to whether or not an individual revision is 'bold' in nature. In keeping with our earlier discussion on herding behavior, a 'bold' analyst is one who revises away from (instead of towards) the pre-existing consensus. In addition, these papers attempt to capture the track record of the analysts whose forecasts make up the consensus, defined along a variety of dimensions, such as their number of years of experience in following the firm or the industry in which it operates, 'all-star' rating status, and the like.

Attempts are underway to construct the ultimate 'smart' consensus forecast that can exploit the timely information and expertise contained in recent forecasts made by specific (skilled) analysts, while reducing the effect of the biases that make them unreliable on a stand-alone basis. Two alternative solutions are possible. One is to identify analysts who might face such conflicts of interest, and omit their forecasts from the aggregate. The second is to include these forecasts in the aggregation process after adjustments for the optimistic bias. These approaches, combined with a consensus based on the revision clusters described earlier, are likely to result in a better proxy for market expectations.

A final caveat in this context relates to whether the consensus earnings forecasts available from commercial services are true measures of the market's expectations, as we have implied so far. An emerging (alternative) measure of earnings expectations is 'whisper' estimates: unofficial forecasts of earnings that circulate among traders and investors. The wide dissemination and popularity of whisper forecasts has been aided by the rapid rise of the Internet as a leading source of investment-related information. Some insight on the influence of whisper numbers is provided by Bagnoli, Beneish, and Watts (1999). They document that, to some extent, the market reaction to earnings announcements appears to be dictated by the direction and magnitude of the surprise in relation to these unofficial forecasts, rather than the surprise calculated from the mean or median of all available forecasts, and that stock prices move when whisper estimates change. However, the evidence on this issue is preliminary, and others (Bhattacharya, Sheikh, and Thiagarajan (2001)) have reached conflicting conclusions.

The other major component in the calculation of earnings surprise, namely, the reported earnings number, has also lost credibility of late, contributing to the decline in the effectiveness of trading strategies based on this metric. As investors have become increasingly focused on whether or not a company meets earnings expectations, the stock price response to earnings surprises has become more swift and more pronounced. In turn, the fear of extreme market consequences has motivated corporate managements to 'manage' both reported earnings numbers and analysts' expectations. A disproportionate number of reported earnings surprises tend to be small positive numbers (as opposed to being negative or zero), presumably because most companies strive to report earnings that have the appearance of beating market (analysts') expectations. The reason these positive surprises tend to be very small in magnitude is that, in many such cases, the cash flows, and hence 'true' earnings of these companies, are not large enough to beat the consensus forecasts. These companies therefore manipulate their accruals to achieve a reported earnings number that meets or exceeds expectations. An alternative (or additional) way of achieving the same outcome is to guide analysts' forecasts down to realistic levels, instead of manipulating the reported earnings number upwards. The recent tendency to provide management guidance is shown by earnings pre-announcements. Recent research in this area indicates that both analysts and investors are becoming increasingly aware of these pitfalls. Large increases in accruals have a beneficial effect on earnings in the short term, but, since accruals reverse in the long term, 'managed' earnings tend to decline and eventually fall below expectations. Analysts are beginning to show some evidence of correcting their subsequent earnings forecasts, and investors are beginning to shy away from rewarding companies following positive earnings surprises, if signs of earnings management, such as a large jump in accruals, are apparent.

International applications

Do earnings surprises matter in international markets? Following the success of earnings surprise models in the U.S. equity markets, it was only a matter of time before academic researchers and investment professionals turned their attention to this issue. A quick and clear answer to this question is clouded by several practical considerations that make it difficult to simply transfer the insights gained from U.S. markets to other markets around the world. We discuss these in turn.

Thus far, our discussion of earnings surprises has not drawn a sharp distinction between annual and quarterly earnings surprises. Although the Ball and Brown study described at the outset of this chapter relates to annual earnings announcements, from an investor's viewpoint, every quarterly earnings announcement represents an opportunity to profit from the mismatch between expectations and outcomes. However, this opportunity is limited by two factors. First, unlike the United States, few countries require companies to report interim results on a quarterly basis.[9] Second, the quality of interim disclosures and earnings estimates varies even in the United States, and the same is likely to be the case in international settings. The reasons for this are not difficult to pinpoint. Analysts' forecast errors are much higher for the fourth interim period. This is because earnings are derived from cash flows and accruals. However, accruals are estimates for the year, and their exact amounts become more certain only as the year progresses. Thus, the fourth quarter likely suffers from a 'settling-up' effect, in that accrual errors of the first three reporting periods are corrected to reflect the correct amount to be accrued for the fiscal year. Indeed, management's leeway in timing of accruals across interim fiscal periods can also translate into delaying bad news until the fourth (last) fiscal period. The consequence of this is that negative earnings surprises in the first three fiscal periods are more 'unexpected' than in the fourth period, and hence the market reaction to fourth quarter negative earnings surprises is greater.

A key issue in the international context is the inherent integrity of earnings forecasts. This depends on the characteristics of the analysts, such as experience, education and incentives, coverage (average number of analysts that follow a typical company), and the like. For example, forecasts from two different sources in Japan (Tokyo Keizai and I/B/E/S) are compared, and the former are more accurate because of differences in the incentive structures at Japanese brokerage houses. Cross-county differences in the degree of agreement in analysts' predictions are a product of cultural diversity. In a study of analysts' forecasts in Canada, Germany, the United Kingdom, and Japan, Rees, Clement, and Swanson (1999) report that analysts employed by the largest brokers had the most accurate forecasts, and that an analyst's experience in following a specific firm and the frequency of forecasts were both positively associated with forecast accuracy.

Another aspect to consider is the effect of international variation in institutional factors, including accounting differences, frequency and usefulness of voluntary disclosures by management, reporting regulations, and average firm size on the forecasts. Of particular interest are the studies conducted on German and Japanese markets. Forecasts in Germany are less accurate than naïve prediction models for longer forecast horizons, and they contain a smaller optimistic bias than forecasts in the United Kingdom. Unlike in the United States, there are no benefits to averaging individual analysts' forecasts in Japan, because there appears to be less unique (analyst-specific) information in individual Japanese forecasts.

The empirical evidence on market reaction to earnings surprises outside the United States is fairly consistent and similar to the U.S. results. In a comprehensive investigation, Bird, McElwee, and McKinnon (2000) examined both the pre-announcement market reaction to earnings surprises and the post-announcement drift in the United States, Canada, and the 19 countries comprising the EAFE Index. They found that in 10 of these countries (Canada, Belgium, Japan, The Netherlands, Sweden, Singapore, the United Kingdom, Hong Kong, Australia, and the United States), there is a significant positive stock price adjustment in anticipation of the earnings surprises. The post-announcement drift was significant on the upside in Belgium and Switzerland, and on the downside in the United Kingdom, the United States, Singapore, and New Zealand. Their study focused on forecasts of annual EPS made about 12 months prior to the earnings announcements. For developed markets, it indicates that trading on a positive earnings surprise strategy has worked consistently well since 1995, but has been effective only since 1998 for negative earnings surprises. Within the developed markets, it has (directionally) performed as expected for both positive and negative surprises in Japan, but only for positive surprises in Europe. In the rest of the Asia–Pacific region, it has performed predictably only for negative surprises. However, the results for emerging markets are mixed, perhaps because the quality of forecast data is much poorer.

More recently, attention has been focused on how companies manage earnings and expectations to achieve desired positive and negative surprises in the United States versus the rest of the world. U.S. managers have greater incentives to enhance their companies' stock prices than do managers in other countries. This is because of greater equity ownership by top executives, more monitoring by institutional shareholders, a larger number of outside directors on their board, a greater threat of external takeovers, and a more litigious environment. Over the period 1976–99 there have been strong changes in the behavior of earnings surprises in the United States, with an increasing number of firms announcing small positive surprises, and in Japan, which has witnessed an increase in negative surprises. The results for Japan, based on data from a shorter time period (1987–99), may be driven by the deteriorating economic conditions in that country.[10] In contrast, while there have been changes in the degree of optimistic bias and dispersion of analysts' forecasts in Europe and Asia, no discernible trend is evident in the frequency or size of small positive or negative surprises.

Portfolio construction issues

Earnings surprises are one of many possible signals that investors take into account when making investment decisions. To the extent other sources convey similar information to market participants, redundancies may arise. Multiple regression models that simultaneously consider the effect of all factors expected to drive stock prices are a popular approach to forecasting returns. A typical problem with such models is the multicollinearity of the various factors. In particular, the direction and magnitude of earnings surprises appear to show a consistent relationship to price momentum variables used in multifactor models. This is not surprising given our previous comments on positive serial correlation among consecutive earnings surprises, post earnings announcement drifts, and the positive relationship between stock prices, forecast revisions, and subsequent earnings surprises. This multicollinearity causes difficulties in the stability and interpretation of regression coefficients. Non-linear approaches, such as cross-classification on factors that might be highly correlated, can help identify stocks for which the correlated signals are confirmatory and thus especially attractive or unattractive.

An important issue that must be considered in constructing portfolios based on earnings surprise models is the weighting scheme for the stocks in the portfolio. Weights based on the relative market capitalization of the desired companies are more appropriate from a risk control point of view. Since most market indices are constructed using the capitalization weight of the component stocks, the relative (benchmark) risk of such an approach is lower. Moreover, it also reduces the absolute risk of the portfolio, in that the quality of both forecast information and reported earnings is higher, and the earnings stream is more stable, for larger companies. However, as we noted in our discussion of the factors affecting the strength of the earnings surprise–stock return relationship, firm size is an important determinant of the market reaction to earnings surprises, and has been shown to vary inversely with market price movements. This situation presents a challenge and a tradeoff to the portfolio manager, who must balance risk and return considerations.

Another problem that mitigates the benefits from trading on earnings surprises of smaller companies is that of liquidity. Shares of smaller companies are typically more illiquid and, depending on the size of the portfolio, a single trade based on an earnings surprise may translate into a large percentage of the stock's normal trading volume or even several days' trading volume. Anticipated gains from earnings surprise strategies may not materialize because of the negative market price impact of building desired positions. While it may be tempting to dodge this problem by taking small positions in several stocks that are attractive from an earnings surprise perspective, trading cost considerations cannot be ignored, especially if active positions are held for short time periods. Indeed, turnover considerations take on even greater importance

Exhibit 12.5

Rank transition matrix

Rows: Ranks of S8Q at t-12. Columns: Ranks of S8Q at t. Ranks = Counts of surprises

		8	7	6	5	4	3	2	1	0
8	Row %	40.4	30.3	17.8	8.6	2.9	0.1			
7	Row %	19.2	27.5	25.7	17.2	7.5	2.9	0.1		
6	Row %	7.9	20.2	25.6	22.4	14.6	7.1	2.1	0.1	
5	Row %	3.3	12.1	21.7	23.1	19.8	13.2	5.4	1.4	0.1
4	Row %	1.1	6.1	14.5	21.9	24.1	17.8	10.0	3.9	0.5
3	Row %	0.0	2.7	9.2	17.3	23.3	23.1	15.0	7.3	2.3
2	Row %		0.0	4.5	11.7	19.1	23.4	22.3	14.0	4.9
1	Row %			0.0	5.6	13.7	20.1	23.2	24.3	13.1
0	Row %				0.2	4.3	10.1	18.0	20.8	46.6

Source: Chicago Investment Analytics (2001).

in attempts to profit from earnings surprise models, because, by their very nature, such models require a reevaluation of the portfolio every time earnings are reported. Taken together with the fact that report dates are clustered in calendar time, this implies a large turnover in portfolio holdings. A recent study by Chicago Investment Analytics (2001) casts some additional light on this issue. The study compares the turnover characteristics of two simple investment strategies based on earnings surprises. At each (quarterly) report date between July 1993 and June 2001, the largest 1,500 stocks in the I/B/E/S database are ranked into (equal-weighted) deciles based on their percentage earnings surprise. The rank transition matrix shown in Exhibit 12.5 indicates the percentage of the original stocks in various deciles 12 months after their initial classification. The numbers suggest, for example, that only 25% of the stocks in the top (most attractive) decile remain in the same decile 12 months later. A naïve trading strategy in which only the top decile is held would thus imply an annual turnover of about 150%.

In contrast, the next transition matrix for an alternative strategy that attempts to take advantage of the serial correlation in earnings surprise suggests that holding a portfolio of stocks that have exhibited eight consistent quarters of positive earnings surprises for a 12 month period results in a somewhat lower turnover of 119.2%.

Exhibit 12.5 compares the information coefficients of the two strategies, leading to the conclusion that the lower turnover does not appear to come at the expense of worse investment performance. However, it is evident from this example that the transaction cost impact of trading on earnings surprises alone is quite high, and that a multifactor approach in which earnings surprises are one of several contributory elements is perhaps more practical.

A final practical issue that must be dealt with in this context is the sector exposure of portfolios built to profit from earnings surprises. We alluded earlier to the commonalities in earnings of companies that belong to the same industry and the phenomenon of intra-industry information transfers. It is not unusual to find that at particular points in the economic cycle, most companies that seem particularly desirable or undesirable based on their earnings surprises belong to the same industry. Taking active positions in all of them can adversely affect the risk characteristics of the portfolio.

Earnings surprise models lend themselves especially well to investment mandates that allow short sales. As various studies have shown, the market reaction to earnings surprises is asymmetric, and 'glamour' stocks are punished especially hard for not meeting expectations. This is because of several reasons. Corporate management tends to delay disclosure of bad news, while good news gradually leaks out during the course of the year, and hence can have a bigger impact upon ultimate disclosure. Exchange traded options are not available for many stocks, and hence opportunities for bad news to price itself fully are restricted. As a result, there are greater opportunities to profit from the pre-earnings announcement drift and the post-announcement reaction to bad news. A popular portfolio management approach is to aim for neutral sector exposures by identifying buy and (short) sell candidates within the same sector.

Summary

When companies 'surprise' analysts, the prices of stocks react quickly. For a portfolio manager using forecasted information, it is essential to understand how 'surprise' works, and to use it to your advantage when picking stocks and building sound portfolios.

References

Bagnoli, M., M.D. Beneish, and S.G. Watts (1999), 'Whisper Forecasts of Quarterly Earnings Per Share', *Journal of Accounting and Economics*, Vol. 28, No. 1, pp. 27–50.

Ball, R., and E. Bartov (1996), 'How Naïve is the Stock Market's Use of Earnings Information?', *Journal of Accounting and Economics*, June, Vol. 21, pp. 319–337.

Ball, R., and P. Brown (1968), 'An Empirical Evaluation of Accounting Income Numbers', *Journal of Accounting Research*, Vol. 6, pp. 159–178.

Basu, S., L. Hwang, and C.L. Jan (1998), 'International Variation in Accounting Measurement Rules and Analysts' Earnings Forecast Errors', *Journal of Business Finance and Accounting*, Vol. 25, Nos 9/10, pp. 1207–1247.

Bernard, V.L., and J.K. Thomas (1990), 'Post-Earnings-Announcement Drift', *Journal of Accounting and Economics*, Vol. 13, pp. 305–340.

Bhattacharya, N., A. Sheikh, and R. Thiagarajan (2001), 'Does the Market Listen to Whispers: An Empirical Investigation of Bias, Accuracy, and Market Perception of Consensus Analyst Forecasts Versus Whisper Forecasts of Earnings?', Working Paper.

Bird, R., B. McElwee, and J. McKinnon (2000), McQuarie Securities newsletter for their clients.

Brown, L.D. (1991), 'Forecast Selection When All Forecasts Are Not Equally Recent', *International Journal of Forecasting*, Vol. 7, No. 3, pp. 349–356.

Brown, L.D. (1997), 'Earnings Surprise Research', *Financial Analysts Journal*, March, Vol. 53, pp. 13–19.

Brown and Chen (1990), 'How Good is the All-America Research Team in Forecasting Earnings?', *Journal of Business Forecasting*, Vol. 9.

Brown, L.D., and S.W. Jeong (1998), 'Profiting from Predicting Earnings Surprise', *Journal of Financial Statement Analysis*, Vol. 4, pp. 57–66.

Brown, L.D., P.A. Griffin, R.L. Hagerman, and M. Zmijewski (1987), 'Security Analyst Superiority Relative to Univariate Time Series Models in Forecasting Quarterly Earnings', *Journal of Accounting and Economics*, April, Vol. 9, pp. 61–81.

Brown, Han, Keon, and Quinn (1996), 'Predicting Analysts' Earnings Surprise', *Journal of Investing*, Vol. 5.

Bhushan, R. (1989), 'Firm Characteristics and Analyst Following', *Journal of Accounting and Economics*, Vol. 11, No. 1, pp. 255–274.

Capstaff, J., K. Paudyal, and W. Rees (1998), 'Analysts' Forecasts of German Firms' Earnings', *Journal of International Financial Management*, Vol. 9, No. 2, pp. 83–116.

Chicago Investment Analytics (2001), newsletter for their clients.

Clement, M. (1999), 'Analyst Forecast Accuracy', *Journal of Accounting and Economics*, Vol. 27, No. 3, pp. 285–303.

Conroy, R.M., R.S. Harris, and Y.S. Park (1994), 'Analysts' Earnings Forecast Accuracy in Japan and the United States', Research Foundation of the ICFA.

Conroy, R.M., R.S. Harris, and Y.S. Park (1998), 'Fundamental Information and Share Prices in Japan: Evidence from Earnings Surprises and Management Predictions', *International Journal of Forecasting*, Vol, 14, No. 2, pp. 227–244.

DeGeorge, F., J. Patel, and R. Zeckhauser (1999), 'Earnings Management to Exceed Thresholds', *Journal of Business*, Vol. 72, No. 1, pp. 1–33.

Dugar, A., and S. Nathan (1995), 'The Effect of Investment Banking Relationships on Financial Analysts Earnings Forecasts and Investment Recommendations', *Contemporary Accounting Research*, Vol. 12, pp. 131–160.

Han, J.C.Y., and J.J. Wild (1990), 'Unexpected Earnings and Intra Industry Information Transfers: Further Evidence', *Journal of Accounting Research*, Vol. 28, No. 1, Spring, pp. 211–219.

Han, J.C.Y., J.J. Wild, and K. Ramesh (1989), 'Managers' Earnings Forecasts and Intra-Industry Information Transfers', *Journal of Accounting and Economics*, Vol. 11, No. 1, pp. 3–33.

Haugen, R.A., and N. Baker (1996), 'Commonality in the Determinants of Expected Stock Return', *Journal of Financial Economics*, Vol. 41, pp. 401–439.

Herzberg, M.M., J. Guo, and L.D. Brown (1999), 'Enhancing Earnings Predictability Using Individual Analyst Forecasts', *Journal of Investing*, Vol. 8, No. 2, pp. 15–24.

Joy, O.M., R.H. Litzenberger, and R.W. McEnally (1977), 'The Adjustment of Stock Prices to Announcements of Unanticipated Changes in Quarterly Earnings', *Journal of Accounting Research*, Vol. 15, No. 2, pp. 207–225.

Lakonishok, J., A. Shliefer, and R.W. Vishny (1994), 'Contrarian Investment, Extrapolation and Risk', *Journal of Finance*, Vol. 49, pp. 1541–1578.

Latane, H.A., and C. Jones (1977), 'Standardized Unexpected Earnings – A Progress Report', *Journal of Finance*, Vol. 32, No. 5, pp. 1457–1465.

Michaely, R., and K.L. Womack (1996), 'Conflict of Interest and the Credibility of Underwriter Analyst Recommendations', Working Paper.

Mozes, H.A., and P.A. Williams (1999), 'Modeling Earnings Expectations Based on Clusters of Analysts Forecasts', *Journal of Investing*, Vol. 8, No. 2, pp. 25–38.

Peters (1993), 'Are Earnings Surprises Predictable?', *Journal of Investing*, Vol. 2.

Ramnath, S. (2000) 'Investor and Analyst Reactions to Earnings Announcements of Related Firms: An Empirical Analysis', *Journal of Accounting Research*, December, Vol. 40, No. 5, pp. 1351–1376.

Rees, L., E.P. Swanson, and M. Clement (1999), 'The Influence of Experience, Resources, and Portfolio Complexity on Analyst Forecast Accuracy in the UK, Germany, Japan, and Canada', Working Paper, August.

Stickel, S.E. (1990), 'Predicting Individual Analyst Earnings Forecasts', *Journal of Accounting Research*, Vol. 28, pp. 409–417.

Wasley, C.E. (2001), 'Information in Externalities Associated With Earnings Pre-announcements', Working Paper.

---

[1] Results for the alternative specification of market expectations (variable 3), based on unexpected earnings derived from the naïve random walk model, were qualitatively similar.

[2] An alternative (statistical) interpretation of the SUE score is that when forecasts are of poor quality, the dispersion among forecasts is likely to be higher, so that the difference between actual and expected earnings is measured with greater error and, consequently, the effect of the surprise on stock prices (for example, in a linear regression) is likely to be smaller.

[3] Excess returns were measured relative to the S&P 500 benchmark.

[4] *Source:* Merrill Lynch private report mailed out by Merrill Lynch in 1999.

[5] *Source*: Marketing materials produced by David Dreman (2002). Reproduced with permission.

[6] Forecast dispersion, measured as the standard deviation of individual analysts' forecasts for a company, has been mentioned as a possible proxy for uncertainty about future earnings in the context of our previous discussion of SUE scores. In addition, the standard deviation of past earnings and the variability of past returns have also been used as measures of uncertainty in past studies. More formalized measures, such as the Value Line earnings predictability index, are also available.

[7] In contrast, a negative forecast is primarily used to persuade existing holders of the stock to sell their holdings, since most individual investors are unwilling to incur the risk of short sales, and many institutional investors are legally prohibited from doing so.

[8] The intra-industry information transfer phenomenon seems pervasive, in that similar associations appear to exist at the time of earnings forecast revisions (Han, Wild, and Ramesh (1989)) and earnings pre-announcements (Wasley (2001)).

[9] Earnings are released on a quarterly basis by Canadian companies, and at six monthly intervals in Japan. Companies in some European countries announce earnings every six months and in others at four month intervals.

[10] In this context, Conroy, Harris, and Park (1998) report that the Japanese stock market appeared to pay less attention to earnings fundamentals, especially during the bubble period of the late 1980s.

Chapter 13

Integrating earnings estimates into a portfolio management strategy

The secret to creativity is knowing how to hide your sources.

Albert Einstein

This book has discussed many facets of earnings and estimates of earnings. The appropriate close to this book is to discuss how to integrate earnings into a portfolio management strategy. One of the most difficult tasks a portfolio manager faces is making his or her product unique. This requires lots of creativity, as so many people utilize a small number of ideas. So Einstein's quote seems appropriate to lead off this chapter – how to make your process unique, while not discussing the sources of your inspiration. In this case, the sources include the hundreds of academic papers that have been written on this subject over many years. Other sources are the dozens of fabulous speakers who have appeared over the years at the Corporate Earnings Analysis Seminar (www. Investmentresearch.org). Additional sources are all of the portfolio managers who have tried to use this data over the years.

So how should we begin with an investment product? First and foremost, one needs an investment philosophy. The philosophy used by the practitioner author is that investors are irrational. However, they are irrational in a consistent manner. Anything done consistently can be taken advantage of. So how are investors irrational? They under-react to new information, and over-react to existing information. An example makes this easy to understand.

A few years ago, Philip Morris was trading at an extreme discount. The price multiples based on tobacco company earnings alone were cheap. The food subsidiary was essentially free. Why did this occur? It was because there was litigation outstanding against the firm. Many smokers' lawsuits were in the courts, and none had been settled. So what was the new information that came into the market? It was the first of the cases being settled. Once those cases were settled, analysts understood earnings would be much stronger than had previously been thought. It took a while for the stock price to react to that information, as Philip Morris had been beaten down for so long, and it was difficult for investors to overcome the psychological bias and invest. When the marketplace finally did react to the information, Philip Morris ended up being one of the best performing stocks in the S&P 500 the following year.

An example of over-reaction occurred during the technology bubble. Cisco is a stock that was in the news daily. It was discussed on TV, in the press, and at cocktail parties. How many people who purchased the stock realized its astronomical valuation ratios? People were buying based on over-reaction to the plethora of news about the firm. Professional investors also held the stock, as who wanted to risk going into a client's office without Cisco in their portfolio and try to explain underperformance?

With this philosophy in mind, how does one integrate earnings estimate data? Previously, we have written in depth about earnings revision and earnings surprise models. How are these models best utilized? Most quantitative investors run regression analysis and determine overall or by sector how much weight to allow each part of their investment process. Take for example a process with only three parts: a security valuation, earnings revision, and price momentum. Our quantitative investor will find that, over time, to create the best forecast of stock returns, the strategy that worked the best is to have some percentage in each of the components. An example would be to have 47% weight to valuation, 26% weight to revisions, and 27% weight to momentum. The problem with this approach is that it does not take into account the over and under reactions that occur, or the proper interaction of factors. When stocks are attractively priced, the amount of momentum they have is not as important as when investors are over reacting to existing information. Upward revisions do not matter as much when valuations are high and momentum is declining. The best use of estimate data is as a gauge of sentiment changes. This is because using analyst data assuming accuracy is wrong. As can be seen from the previously shown study done by David Dreman (1998), analyst estimates are wrong by an average of 41%. So how do you best use analyst data? We are going to look at the example of small cap stocks: first, looking at how small caps are unique, and then at how to put revisions into the complete process.

A large amount of literature has accumulated over the years on various forms of 'small-cap effects' that summarize a number of apparent systematic differences in the behavior of stock returns of small-capitalization stocks versus that of large-capitalization stocks. While such effects have been used in many different kinds of stock return forecasting models, perhaps the most important of which is based on the standard Fama-French factor model,[1] it is interesting to note that relatively little attention has been given to the problem of forecasting stock returns within the small-stock universe.

We find that the results of valuation research that has been mainly conducted on either a purely large cap universe or the entire market translate to the small-cap-only realm with a number of important differences. In particular, the problem of stock selection within the small-cap universe presents an interesting dilemma in terms of the data available. While it has been pointed out that market inefficiencies (if any) are likely to be larger in the small-cap universe, thus allowing for more profitable forecasting strategies, the very lack of widely available and timely information that drives these inefficiencies makes quantitative modeling more difficult. In this context of slower information diffusion and lower data availability, we argue that the data needs to be processed with special attention to extreme cases, where the lack of timely and in-depth information may generate particularly large pricing inefficiencies.

Our findings show that while the standard linear way in which many variables are used in return forecasting and stock-picking models tends to be correct for most observations, within the small-cap universe the extremes tend to break those trends, sometimes in a fairly dramatic way. While this trend-breaking phenomenon is in evidence on a wider range of variables, we have picked a short list of examples with which to demonstrate the importance of this effect.

Four key small cap extremes: extreme data, extreme price, extreme value, and extreme debt

This chapter examines four distinct extremes: extreme data, extreme price, extreme value, and extreme debt. We start the next section with the most obvious case, that of the extreme of data availability itself, where the behavior of returns is considered when there is no data at all. In the section after that, we consider the most basic piece of information available about a stock: its price level. We show that while the price of a stock itself should be irrelevant, the low end of the scale can be quite useful in reflecting the market's negative view of small-cap firms. The third factor we examine is the widely used book-to-market ratio. We show that an aggressive value strategy performs perversely if the investor does not account for the possibility that high book-to-market stocks may be correctly priced at those low values. The construction of a version of the book-to-market factor that incorporates additional pricing information at the cheap end of the valuation spectrum can be quite simple, and requires no more than the use of standard multidimensional diagnostic tools. Finally, we use the debt ratio as a proxy for the market's confidence in the future of a firm. While this factor is effective in the small cap universe, it needs to be modified to account for those firms with extreme debt equity ratios. The results in each case are interesting, and, we believe, illustrate not only an important difference in the behavior of returns between small and large cap firms, but also provide some guidance in how to adapt very standard modeling and diagnostic techniques to the small-cap arena.

All of our results are based on monthly data collected from January 1990 to December 2002, adding up to 144 monthly periods. Total return data, I/B/E/S coverage data, and Valueline Financial data was collected for all Russell 2000 (hereafter the R2K universe) constituents throughout that period.

Extreme data: when lack of data is informational

The first extreme we examine is the extreme of data availability itself. In particular, we look at the possibility that missing data is a systematic extreme event that can, in fact, be used as a signal of unusual performance expectations.

In any asset pricing and forecasting research, the availability and quality of data is the basic constraint on what kind of market dynamics can be considered, the complexity of the model to be used, the type of econometric technique to be applied, and the level of pricing, forecast, or portfolio formation frequencies that can be supported. The handling of missing data is thus a topic that has got a fair amount of attention, on issues ranging from survivor bias to regression analysis when missing data is present. This chapter focuses on two basic cases of missing data: the lack of analyst coverage, and the lack of timely financial data. The first case has been extensively studied (though not in the context of a small-cap only universe) as a source of information on systematic performance differences across firms, while the second case has generally been viewed simply as a limit on what could be modeled, rather than as a source of additional information.

To illustrate the potential importance of accounting for I/B/E/S coverage dynamics during small-cap modeling, consider the availability of I/B/E/S analyst forecasts within the Russell 3000 universe as of January 2003. The large cap portion (the Russell 1000, hereafter R1K) has some I/B/E/S coverage for all but 5% of its constituents, adding up to over 98% of its total capitalization. On the other hand, the small-cap portion (the Russell 2000) has no I/B/E/S coverage for a full 20% of its constituents, adding up to over 15% of its total capitalization.

While it appears intuitive that profitable (information-inefficiency related) opportunities may exist for stock picking companies that have no analyst coverage, we find that at the aggregate level stocks with no coverage under perform those that have analyst coverage. Exhibit 13.1 shows that, for the period under consideration, non-covered firms have monthly

Exhibit 13.1

I/B/E/S coverage effect

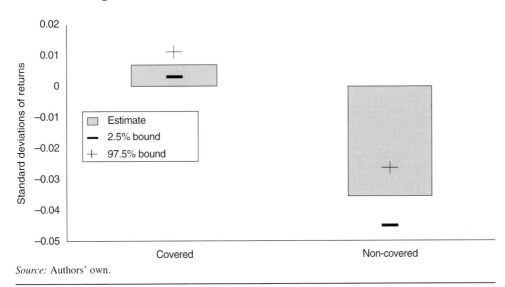

Source: Authors' own.

Exhibit 13.2

I/B/E/S coverage portfolio value added summary (annualized)

	Covered	*Non-covered*
Mean	1.04	−4.57
Standard	1.59	7.79
Ratio	0.66	−0.59
Mean difference test, p-value		0.0146
JK Ratio test, p-value		0.0118

[a] Standard t-test (1-sided) conducted on zero-mean hypothesis for the difference in monthly value added between covered and non-covered portfolios.

[b] Standard Jobson-Korkie test (1-sided).

Source: Authors' own.

returns about 0.04 standard deviations lower than covered firms. This difference is statistically significant at the 5% level[2] and can, in fact, be large. For example, in 2002 the standard deviation of returns in the industrials sector was around 14% per month, thus making our estimated 0.04 gap equivalent to an annualized return difference of close to 2%.

To see if these estimates translate into actual portfolio performance differences, Exhibit 13.2 summarizes the result of building portfolios of non-covered firms and comparing them with those of covered firms. It can be seen that non-covered firms have annualized value added of about 5% less than covered firms, plus significantly higher standard deviations. It is important to note that not only is the value added difference significant at the 5% level, but the difference in information ratios is also significant at the 5% level. This is notable because,

Exhibit 13.3

Cumulative value added – I/B/E/S covered versus non-covered portfolios, February 1990 to February 2002

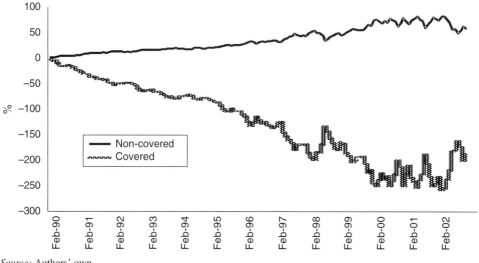

Source: Authors' own.

using the standard Jobson-Korkie, test it is generally difficult to obtain such a result unless information ratio differences are quite large. The result thus provides very strong evidence that the underperformance of companies with no coverage is highly systematic. Exhibit 13.3 shows that these performance differences imply very large cumulative value added differences over the period under consideration.

A similar analysis within the R1K universe reveals that no-coverage (or little-coverage) firms do not experience the same systematic negative effect. The standard behavioral explanation for this difference, as documented above, is that analysts have an incentive (due to compensation and career concerns, as well as due to time and data constraints) to be selective in the number of companies they cover within the small cap universe. Within the large cap universe, however, such incentives are smaller in comparison with the need to cover large, liquid, and well-known firms. Given this incentive, it is natural to assume that they use their presumably superior experience and information to cover only those firms expected to be better performing. We summarize this behavioral hypothesis here, because any effort to pick stocks among those that have no analyst coverage will be at least partially based on standardized financial data mechanically collected and delivered by one of many data-delivery companies. It is not unreasonable to assume that the kind of incentives that apply to analysts submitting reports to the I/B/E/S service do not apply to the staff of firms whose business is to collect and deliver reported financial data. We test this assumption below, using the Valueline financials database, one of the most widely used sources of reported financial data in the U.S. market.

Using the Valueline database, we find that complete and timely financial data is not available for a number of firms within the small-cap universe. In particular, during the period under consideration, there is an average of slightly over 200 firms per month for which no full and timely set of Valueline financials is available. These companies represent an average of slightly over 10% of the total market capitalization of the R2K. It should be noted, moreover, that, of

118

Exhibit 13.4

Valueline missing-data portfolio value-added summary (annualized)

	Non-missing	Missing
Mean	1.64	−9.75
Standard	1.17	8.02
Ratio	1.40	−1.22
Mean difference test, p-value		0.0000
JK Ratio test, p-value		0.0000

[a] Standard t-test (1-sided) conducted on zero-mean hypothesis for the difference in monthly value added between covered and non-covered portfolios.
[b] Standard Jobson-Korkie test (1-sided).

Source: Authors' own.

those firms that have missing Valueline financials, only about half have no I/B/E/S coverage. Similarly, only about half of the total weight of missing-data firms in the R2K comes from the bottom half of the R2K universe (by value). This implies that traditional analyst coverage and firm size are not, in fact, the main drivers of Valueline coverage choices, and that any missing data effects observed using the Valueline database are not wholly explained by either the I/B/E/S coverage effect documented above or a systematic firm-size effect.

Exhibits 13.4, 13.5, and 13.6 summarize the results of conducting the same series of tests done on the availability of I/B/E/S coverage with our Valueline data. It is immediately clear that the Valueline missing data effect is not only statistically significant on all counts, but also much larger than that observed for the case of I/B/E/S coverage. Indeed, the effect gap

Exhibit 13.5

Cumulative value added – Valueline missing versus non-missing portfolios, February 1990 to February 2002

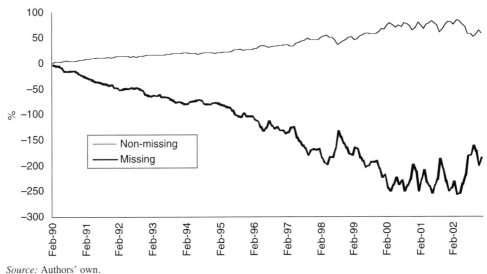

Source: Authors' own.

Exhibit 13.6

Stock price decile analysis – R2K universe

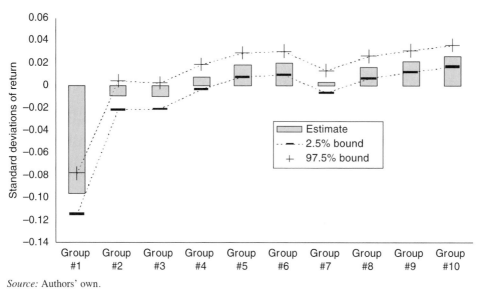

Source: Authors' own.

between missing-data and non-missing-data firms is close to 0.09 standard deviations, more than double than that obtained in the I/B/E/S case. Similarly, the annualized value added difference in our rolling portfolio test was over 10%, again more than double than that obtained in the I/B/E/S case. As was the case above, a similar test conducted within the R1K universe reveals that this large missing data effect is not reliably present within large-cap stocks.

These results clearly contradict the assumption that missing data effects should not reflect return differentials because analyst-type incentives are not present when considering reported financial data only. While it is clear that the marginal cost of additional coverage by a large data provider such as Valueline should be lower than that of additional coverage by an analyst, other considerations in their coverage choices must, in fact, be systematically linked to a firm's performance. Linkages between the data providers' pure data collection operations and their index and forecast operations may play a significant role.[3] It would appear, in any case, that the same care with which the dynamics of analyst coverage has been studied needs to be given to the dynamics of data providers' coverage choices.

In summary, the results show that any attempt at identifying attractive small-cap stocks among those that have no analyst coverage or no timely financial data needs to overcome not only the usual difficulties of any stock-picking effort, but also the systematic lower returns associated with no-data stocks. The inclusion of this 'missing data penalty' is thus clearly important in any small-cap forecasting of portfolio construction process.

Extreme price: low price, bad news

Having considered the effects of missing data, both in terms of analyst coverage and financials coverage, we move to our second extreme data example, based on the most basic piece of information available about a stock: its price level. The reason the use of price as a forecasting or portfolio con-

Exhibit 13.7

Stock price decile analysis – R1K universe

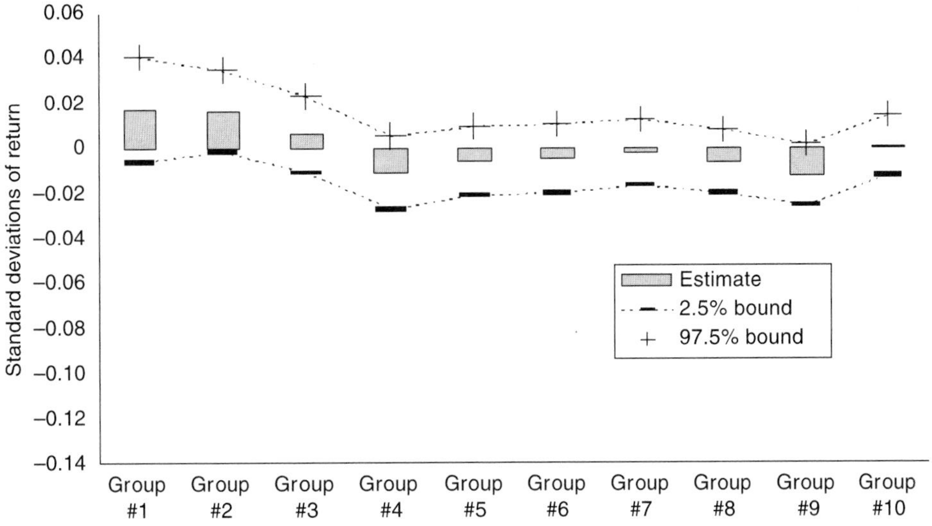

Source: Authors' own.

struction factor is interesting is that, in principle, a stock's price level should be irrelevant. Indeed, theory tells us that price changes, independently of level, should reflect all information flow. Of course, it is clear that most stock markets do not conform to the many assumptions that are generally used to derive the theoretical properties of stock price behavior: stocks do not trade continuously, price 'ticks' are coarse, trade costs and liquidity risks can be significant, and the like. In addition, it has become more and more clear that perfect rationality on the part of investors is not always a reasonable assumption. Indeed, a recent report conducted by Standard & Poor's (2002) concludes that low-price stocks 'are more volatile, have higher transaction costs, have thinner markets, and may also be subject to peculiar behavior coming out of investor psychology'.

Do these issues translate into a systematic data regularity that can be used to pick stocks? Exhibit 13.6 shows the decile analysis plot for the stock price itself, when restricted to the R2K universe. While most of the range shows no clear relationship between price level and return, the lowest decile is linked to large negative mean standardized returns,[4] with the difference between the 1st and 2nd deciles very large, and statistically significant at the 5% level. In contrast, Exhibit 13.7 shows the same plot for the R1K universe. The effect is not in evidence at all, with all deciles not significantly different from zero. It appears, then, that the intuition that the price level itself is irrelevant is reflected only in data for large cap companies. In the small cap universe, however, low price levels appear to reflect several possible violations to the standard efficient market hypothesis. Among these, the effect may be the reflection of additional costs of trading in small low-priced securities, the result of price levels acting as signals for negative information when a stock is thinly traded, or a more complex behavioral effect that links low price with a perception of low quality for stocks about which little widely distributed additional information is available.

Exhibit 13.8 shows the rolling portfolio cumulative value added of the 1st price decile and the rest of the universe versus the entire R2K universe, demonstrating that the poten-

Exhibit 13.8

Cumulative value added – low raw price versus rest of the universe, February 1990 to February 2002

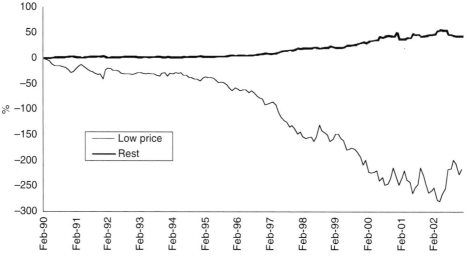

Source: Authors' own.

Exhibit 13.9

Low price versus rest – value added summary (annualized)

	Low price	Rest of the universe
Mean	−8.46	0.92
Standard	25.68	2.76
Ratio	−0.33	0.33
Mean difference test, p-value	0.1179	
JK Ratio test, p-value	0.1181	

[a] Standard t-test (1-sided) conducted on zero-mean hypothesis for the difference in monthly value added between covered and non-covered portfolios.
[b] Standard Jobson-Korkie test (1-sided).

Source: Authors' own.

tial effect of investing in the two separate groups of stocks can be quite large. A more detailed evaluation of the statistical significance of these differences can be found in Exhibit 13.9. The mean value added difference between the two groups is very large (at more than 8%, annualized), with value added volatility dramatically larger for the low-price group. Given these large standard deviation differences, it is notable that the formal tests for differences-in-means and information ratio differences are still close to the 10% significance level.

From the modeling point of view, this 'low price' effect can be quite easily included in many different types of decision processes. In fact, one can take this procedure to its own extreme and simply 'filter' all data under consideration through any number of flexible fitting procedures (among others, nonparametric regression, wavelet fitting, and neural networks) without regard for financial or economic intuition. In the next two sections, we show that exploring and incorporating data nonlinearities in the behavior of small cap stocks need not take the form of 'black box' modeling. It can be useful not just in increasing the fit of our models, but also in sharpening out intuition about the source of these nonlinearities.

Extreme value: cheap for a reason

The next extreme we examine is that of extreme valuations. Since the 1960s, a wide array of studies have looked at the effectiveness of using standard valuation measures as the basis for investing. In an interesting short survey, Dreman (1998) looks at studies by Nicholson, Basu, Fama and French, and Lakonishok, Shleifer, and Vishny, and shows that these valuation-based strategies do appear to have continued success. More recently, Piotroski (2000) finds that simple combinations of valuation measures can be used to consistently identify better-performing stocks and form superior portfolio strategies. In work more closely related to our sector-neutral analysis, Dreman and Lufkin (1997) reach similar conclusions, but based on a framework in which valuation effects are considered within separate industry groups.

Among the many widely used valuation measures, perhaps the most popular is the book-to-market ratio, which is intended to reflect the market's view of the intrinsic linkage between a firm's accounting value and its ability to generate earnings. As a fundamental building block of the Fama and French (1992) family of models, the book-to-market ratio is used in countless asset pricing models both in the financial industry as well as in the academic community. Leaving aside the large empirical literature on whether or not the existence of a book-to-market effect can be statistically confirmed, the book-to-market factor is popular partly because it can be explained by a simple mean-reversion argument. In particular, given some average 'normal' ability to generate profit from a given level of book value, it seems natural to expect that, in the long run, firms that have low book-to-market valuations would eventually catch up with firms priced at the normal level. The opposite would be expected for firms priced at higher-than-normal levels.

The application of this intuition generally takes the form of a linear factor model where book-to-market measurements are used without any transformations. As is shown in Exhibit 13.10, we find that, while an overall linear relationship appears to exist between returns and the various decile groups of the book-to-market ratio, the cheapest end shows a marked break of trend for small cap securities. In particular, the mean standardized return for the cheapest group is as low as that of the middle group, and is, in fact, statistically different (at the 5% level) from that of the 9th decile. Exhibit 13.11 shows the result of using the same deciles to construct rolling portfolios. A similar behavior is clearly visible: the cheap end of the scale breaks the monotonic increasing relationship apparent in the rest of the range of the book-to-market variable. The break is large enough to cause an information ratio difference between the 9th and 10th deciles that is significant at the 5% level. It appears, then, that a very aggressive value strategy within the small cap universe, where the cheapest stocks are over weighted, would be counterproductive. The standard linear factor setup is, in fact, inappropriate for such a strategy. Moreover, a similar analysis within the large cap universe reveals that the relationship between book-to-market and return is not only less strong, but the 'break' is not statistically important.

Exhibit 13.10

Book-to-market decile analysis

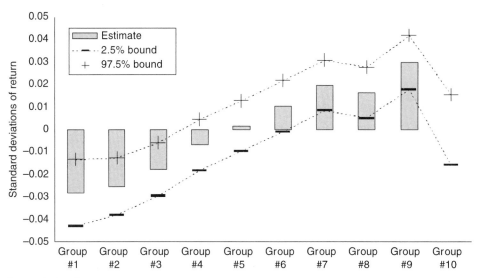

Source: Authors' own.

Exhibit 13.11

Book-to-market rolling portfolios

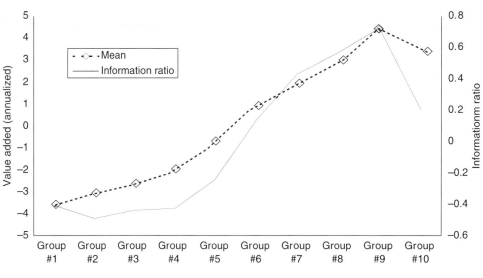

Source: Authors' own.

As was suggested for the 'low price' effect, we could simply incorporate this nonlinearity in the book-to-market effect and leave it at that. However, we do not want to give up the potential for higher returns that can accrue from distinguishing the true value stocks in this extreme group from those that are correctly priced at a low level. The question is, then, whether we can build a model that is successful at separating those stocks that are good values, as opposed to those that are 'cheap for a reason'.

To answer this question, we focused on one of the major reasons why a firm may have (justified) low valuations: the possibility of future financial distress. The intuition behind why cheap small cap stocks may be more likely to have financial problems and be less able to weather such problems is fairly straightforward. First, smaller capitalization firms generally have a limited number of products and/or geographic coverage. Second, smaller firms generally find it more difficult to find financing opportunities, either in terms of direct investment or via the issuance of debt. If a small firm with a limited product line experiences any serious competitive challenge, it may not be able to stay in business. As an example, consider a firm that manufactures disk drives. If a competitor enters the market with a drive that is 10 times as fast at half the cost, unless the small firm has a new product or geographic market ready to launch, the competing product will gain the majority of market share, and drive the small firm into bankruptcy. This effect is clearly not as pronounced with larger firms, since they generally have a more diversified operation. Similarly, large firms also have more ability to raise debt and equity capital via their more extended banking and investment banking relationships. These financing opportunities can clearly make the difference between successful operations and bankruptcy for a small firm under stress.

In order to model financial distress, we combined some of the research that has been conducted on bankruptcy forecasting with that of more traditional return forecasting. In particular, we constructed a series of 'bankruptcy scores' modeled along the lines proposed by Altman (1968, 2000) and Altman, Haldeman, and Narayanan (1977) as a way of measuring the probability of financial distress. These scores can then serve as a sieve among those firms with very low valuations: if a firm has a low valuation but does not appear to have a high probability of financial distress, then we expect its returns to behave according to the typical monotone increasing relationship between book-to-market and return, rather than exhibit the trend break that is observed in Exhibits 13.11 and 13.12.

The bankruptcy score (hereafter z-score) used in this study was constructed as a blend of several standard accounting ratios, similar to those used by Piotroski (2000). To maintain consistency with the cross-sectional sector-neutral framework used throughout this piece, the components of the score were all constructed to be sector and time-neutral. Lower values of z-score indicate higher probability of financial distress and, eventually, bankruptcy.[5]

Exhibit 13.12 looks at whether or not this bankruptcy score setup is effective in distinguishing among cheap stocks. In particular, we estimated mean standardized return across both the book-to-market and the z-score dimensions, in essence a three-dimensional version of the decile analysis conducted above. It can be seen that the monotone relationship between book-to-market and return holds for higher levels of z-score, but becomes concave for low values of z-score. That is, cheap firms with higher probabilities of financial distress appear to suffer from the 'cheap for a reason' problem, whereas similarly cheap companies under no risk of financial distress (as measured by the z-score) do not. Based on this result, we propose the use of an 'enhanced' book-to-market effect where observations that fall in the high book-to-market and low z-score quadrant of Exhibit 13.12 are treated differently from those in the 'main' group of observations.

For a more detailed evaluation of the effectiveness of using the z-score in the high end of book-to-market, consider performing decile analysis and rolling portfolio analysis with this modified version of book-to-market variable. Exhibit 13.13 shows that, while the mod-

Exhibit 13.12

Book-to-market versus bankruptcy score

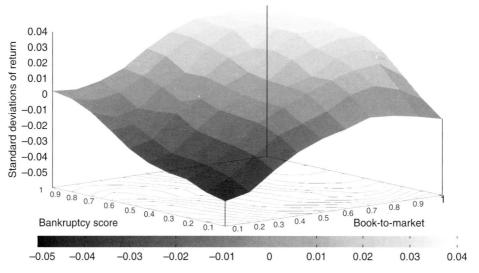

Source: Authors' own.

Exhibit 13.13

Modified book-to-market decile analysis

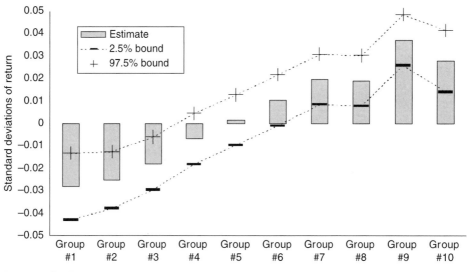

Source: Authors' own.

ified version is not perfectly linear, the sharp break observed for the least expensive stocks is no longer nearly as dramatic as it was in the unmodified case.[6] In particular, notice that the 10th decile is no longer statistically different from the preceding decile, and that a linear trend line lying within the confidence bounds can be traced along the entire range of deciles.

Exhibit 13.14

Cumulative value added book-to-market 10th decile unmodified versus modified, February 1990 to February 2002

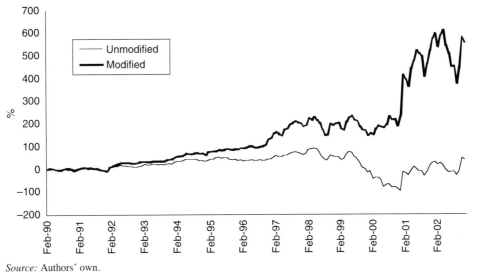

Source: Authors' own.

Exhibit 13.15

Book-to-market 10th decile (annualized) value added summary – unmodified versus modified results

	Unmodified	*Modified*
Mean	3.44	8.81
Standard	16.93	11.08
Ratio	0.20	0.79
Mean difference test, p-value		0.0238
JK Ratio test, p-value		0.0001

[a] Standard t-test (1-sided) conducted on zero-mean hypothesis for the difference in monthly value added between covered and non-covered portfolios.

[b] Standard Jobson-Korkie test (1-sided).

Source: Authors' own.

The modified version is, then, a better fit with traditional linear factor modeling than is its unmodified variant.

To see the difference between the behavior of the 10th decile for the unmodified and modified cases, consider comparing the 10th decile rolling portfolio of the unmodified case with that of the modified portfolio, where rolling portfolio weights are based on how close each observation in the 10th decile is to the extreme of the low z-score and high book-to-market quadrant. The results can be seen in Exhibit 13.14 and 13.15. It is clear that the portfolio-level effect of the modification can be quite large, with statistically significant annualized value-added differences of close to 5%, as well as large and statistically significant information ratio differences.

In summary, it appears that the standard use of the book-to-market ratio as a valuation tool within the small cap universe needs to be modified to take into account the possibility that very low-valued stocks are correctly valued at such low levels due to, among other possibilities, concerns about financial viability. Given the simplicity of the setup, it is notable how effective it can be, both as a way of understanding the dynamics of the data as well as a way of building portfolios.

Extreme debt: debt as a proxy for confidence

Our final extreme is that of extreme debt levels, where we examine the effects of too much debt on thinly capitalized small cap firms. In an environment where data on the prospects of a firm is not widely available, we think it natural to look at the debt market for a proxy of what level of performance is expected of a firm. As we noted in the previous section, financing opportunities are generally smaller for firms within the small cap universe, and can thus be expected to be of significant importance in determining their success. Indeed, we expect that firms whose prospects have been recognized as promising will more likely carry higher levels of debt to finance their operations and leverage their earnings.

If the use of this variable seems natural, we should ask why it is generally not used in traditional factor models of stock return.[7] To answer this question, we can quote Piotrosky (2000), who includes leverage as a negative signal in his setup: 'since most high book-to-market firms are financially constrained, it is assumed that an increase in leverage, deterioration of liquidity or the use of external financing is a bad signal about financial risk.' The intuitive flaw in the debt ratio as a factor in return modeling is, then, that while higher levels of debt do multiply a firm's return and possibly act as a proxy for confidence in the firm's future, it also implies higher levels of risk, and thus is clearly detrimental if taken to extremes. In other words, a non-linear relationship between this factor and return is to be expected, and thus it is not easily incorporated in traditional linear factor models.

The debt ratio, however, fits the framework used in the previous section, where a factor with a monotone relationship with return that reverses at an extreme of its range requires an adjustment to separate observations correctly priced at lower (trend-breaking) levels from those where the factor is still usable. Exhibit 13.16 and 13.17 confirm the first part of the setup: higher levels of debt have indeed some forecasting power for return, except at the extreme, with the 9th and 10th deciles in Exhibit 13.17 reversing the monotone increasing trend. A similar shape is evident in the value added and information ratio numbers from the rolling portfolio tests used to build Exhibit 13.18.

What can play the role of a modifier for large debt levels, such as the role of the bankruptcy score used in the previous section? We find that, while in-depth debt evaluation is a complex process, in the small cap universe the most important consideration when evaluating whether a given level of debt ratio is 'too high' is the size of the firm itself. The intuition for this is two-fold. First, smaller firms are less able to weather downturns in their business when carrying large debt burdens, since it is more difficult for them to reduce costs, raise prices, and find alternatives or additional financing opportunities. Second, the size of a firm can also serve as a long-term market measure of a firm's success vis-à-vis its debt level, since any firm that takes a large debt burden to finance an expansion or investment that it does not

Exhibit 13.16

Debt ratio decile analysis

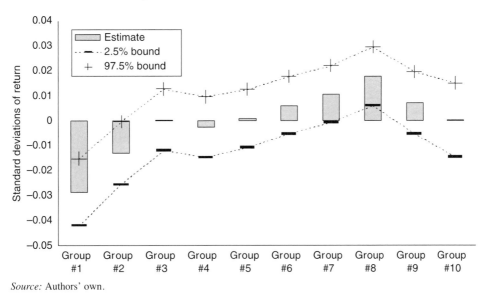

Source: Authors' own.

Exhibit 13.17

Debt ratio rolling portfolios

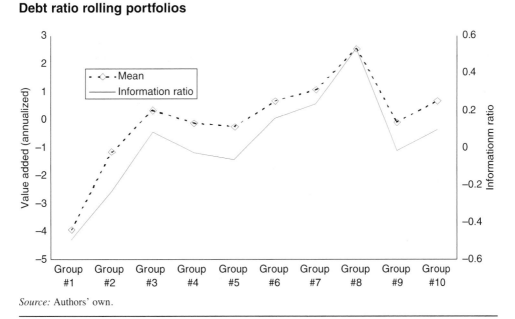

Source: Authors' own.

pay off will eventually be punished for failure via its market price, and thus its capitalization.[8] Exhibit 13.18 shows that this intuition is reflected in the data: the two-dimensional response surface depicts a fully monotone relationship between debt ratio and return for the larger firms in the universe, whereas a clearly concave relationship is evident for those firms at the

Exhibit 13.18

Debt ratio versus market capitalization

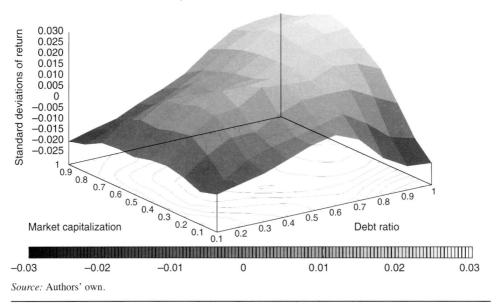

Source: Authors' own.

Exhibit 13.19

Modified debt ratio decile analysis

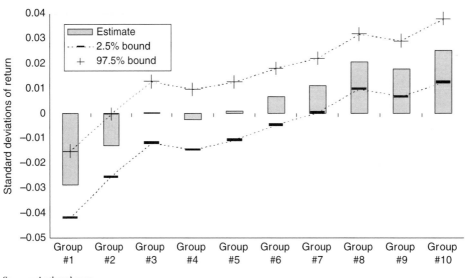

Source: Authors' own.

lower end of the capitalization scale of the R2K universe. The plot is, in fact, a more dramatic example of non-linear dependence than that observed in the previous section.

Using a scheme similar to that used when adjusting book-to-market with the bankruptcy score, we generated a modified debt ratio factor, with its decile analysis results

Exhibit 13.20

Cumulative value added debt ratio 10th decile unmodified versus modified, February 1990 to February 2002

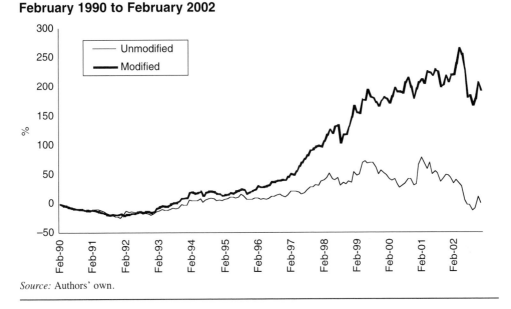

Source: Authors' own.

Exhibit 13.21

Debt ratio 10th decile (annualized) value added summary: unmodified versus modified results

	Unmodified	*Modified*
Mean	0.69	3.69
Standard	7.13	5.78
Ratio	0.10	0.64
Mean difference test, p-value		0.0662
JK Ratio test, p-value		0.0390

[a] Standard t-test (1-sided) conducted on zero-mean hypothesis for the difference in monthly value added between covered and non-covered portfolios.
[b] Standard Jobson-Korkie test (1-sided).

Source: Authors' own.

plotted in Exhibit 13.19. The last two deciles now conform to the general linear relationship between debt ratio and return, reducing the risk of inappropriate use of this factor during stock-picking. A comparison of the rolling portfolio performance of the 10th decile portfolios of the unmodified and modified versions of the debt ratio factor yields a result similar to that observed in the previous section. In particular, Exhibits 13.20 and 13.21 show that the 10th decile annualized performance gap between the unmodified and modified cases is close to 3% (significant at the 5% level), with information ratio differences equally large.

Exhibit 13.22

Investment process

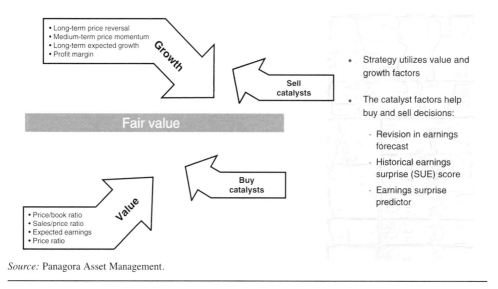

- Long-term price reversal
- Medium-term price momentum
- Long-term expected growth
- Profit margin

Growth

Sell catalysts

Fair value

Buy catalysts

Value

- Price/book ratio
- Sales/price ratio
- Expected earnings
- Price ratio

- Strategy utilizes value and growth factors

- The catalyst factors help buy and sell decisions:
  - Revision in earnings forecast
  - Historical earnings surprise (SUE) score
  - Earnings surprise predictor

Source: Panagora Asset Management.

In summary, it is clear that the overall effectiveness of the debt ratio factor can be significantly enhanced using a simple market cap based adjustment at the top of the scale, especially if the factor is to be used in a standard linear model setup.

Putting it all together

The first thing you want to do is find stocks that are good value. We have seen from the above research what needs to be examined in the small cap universe. Now that we have determined what is an attractively priced security, we need to make sure the timing of the buy is right. This is the key to using earnings estimates. They are demonstrated to be inaccurate, but they do indicate sentiment changes. Remember our philosophy that we are looking for new information flowing into the marketplace that investors are under-reacting to. This is where you should look at things like earnings revisions (see Exhibit 13.22). This helps in timing investments better. Value managers buy cheap stocks, but tend to hold them for long periods before the price reacts. This is because, until the market recognizes a stock is mis-priced, the price will not move. Using estimate data to time the purchase and sale of securities is the key to using them properly.

Summary

In building portfolios, investors would be wise to include estimate data. We have examined in this chapter one example of how to incorporate that data into an investment process. We realize that data are always inaccurate. The inaccuracy doesn't matter. What matters is the sentiment that the estimate changes convey. A sound approach is to start with valuation information. It has been proven over many decades of academic studies to be a valid investment principle. The insights gleaned from the rise of behavioral finance can be used to properly time buys, when to hold and when to sell. Analyst data is the key to understanding how investor's sentiment is changing. Using that sentiment properly should be a key component to any good investment philosophy.

References

Altman, E. (1968), 'Financial Ratios, Discriminant Analysis and the Prediction of Corporate Bankruptcy', *Journal of Finance,* Vol. 23, pp. 589–609.

Altman, E., R. Haldeman, and P. Narayanan (1977), 'Zeta Analysis: A New Model to Identify Bankruptcy Risk of Corporations', *Journal of Banking & Finance,* Vol. 1, pp. 29–51.

Altman, E. (2000), 'Predicting Financial Distress of Companies: Revisiting the Z-score and Zeta® Models', unpublished Working Paper (July).

Davis, J.L., E.F. Fama, and K.R. French (2000), 'Characteristics, Covariances, and Average Returns: 1929 to 1997', *Journal of Finance,* Vol. 55, pp. 389–406.

Dreman, D., and E. Lukfin (1997), 'Do Contrarian Strategies Work Within Industries?', *Journal of Investing*, Vol. 6, No. 3, pp. 7–29.

Dreman, D. (1998), *Contrarian Investment Strategies: The Next Generation*, New York, Simon & Schuster, pp. 139–159.

Fama, E.F., and K.R. French (1992), 'The Cross-Section of Expected Stock Returns', *Journal of Finance*, Vol. 47, pp. 427–465.

Härdle, W. (1990), *Applied Nonparametric Regression*, Cambridge, Cambridge University Press.

Jobson, J. D., and B.M. Korkie (1981), 'Performance Hypothesis Testing with the Sharpe and Treynor Measures', *Journal of Finance,* Vol. 36, pp. 889–908.

Pagan, A., and A. Ullah (1999), *Nonparametric Econometrics*, Cambridge, Cambridge University Press.

Piotroski, J. (2000), 'Value Investing: The Use of Historical Financial Statement Information to Separate Winners from Losers', *Journal of Accounting Research,* Vol. 38 (Supplement), pp. 1–41.

Standard & Poor's (2002), *Low Price Stocks: Key Characteristics and an Indexing Perspective*, Standard & Poor's Index Analysis Reports, 4 October.

---

[1] See Fama and French (1992). For a more recent review of related literature, see Davis, Fama, and French (2000).

[2] Given that in this setup the dummy variables used to estimate the mean effect by group are orthogonal by definition, a test on the hypothesis that the effects are equal to each other can be conducted via checking whether or not their confidence intervals overlap.

[3] Valueline not only provides financial data, but also maintains a number of price indices and a series of publications that provide company outlooks as well as forecasts for a wide number of financial variables.

[4] It is important to note that this effect is not related to the scale variations in the market either across time or across sector groups, since the decile groups are formed cross-sectionally within sector.

[5] It should be noted that the actual value of the scores are, in our setup, irrelevant, since their usage is intended to be relative to other stocks within a sector and a time period.

[6] The general nature of this result is robust to the details of the construction of our modified factor. The specific estimates will of course change depending on how large and smooth the 'cheap for a reason' region is defined.

[7] The debt ratio is widely used in other contexts, in particular the traditional DuPont analysis for the evaluation of a firm's operations.

[8] It is important to remark that, as described in the introduction, all of our analysis is done in a cross-sectional, sector-neutral framework. It is thus not the case that capitalization reductions (or increases) that are sector-wide or market-wide will affect the debt-ratio versus capitalization dynamics described here. It is, in fact, the relative level of capitalization that is important in this case.

Chapter 14

Conclusion

A great book should leave you with many experiences, and slightly exhausted at the end.

William Styron

By no means do we believe that this is a great book. We hope it was a useful book, and that you have gained some insight into how earnings and earnings estimates are created and utilized. Further, it is our hope that you will not be exhausted but invigorated by the discussions and ideas included in this book.

The study of finance typically deals with analysis and interpretation of historical and contemporaneous information. The collection of estimate data is unique in that it is a window on current expectations that is not covered by any other data collected. Professors for years have used data feeds like the one from the University of Chicago's Center for Research in Security Prices to create event studies based on historical data. This knowledge was critical in collecting facts about security returns and for looking at pricing of securities in markets. What these inquiries lacked was any behavioral component. This lead to theories, like the efficient market hypothesis, which is based on rationality. Without information on expectations, there is no way to judge if market participants are acting in any way but rationally. The creation of the I/B/E/S database finally allowed finance researchers to examine market sentiment before informational flows, and therefore allowed us an insight into rationality.

The topics covered in this book are really the first event studies of behavioral finance. Behavioral finance combines the fields of psychology and finance. It allows finance professionals for the first time to understand why anomalies in the efficient market hypothesis occur. Prices do deviate from fair value. Over and under reactions do occur. Since the introduction of the term 'over-reaction' over two decades ago to describe systematic behavior, it has come to have a very broad meaning, and now seems to be a catchall explanation of market anomalies. The explanation for this phenomenon follows from the hypothesis that the mispricing is based on investors' perceptions.

The problem that behavioral finance has wrestled with is the lack of data from which to study the effects of perception in the markets. Most of the early studies focused on theories and did not have event studies associated with them. Researchers then found two profitable areas for event studies: expectational earnings data and laboratory experiments. I/B/E/S started collecting data from analysts many years ago. By the 1990s, the dataset had a long history and covered most large companies in the marketplace. This data allowed event studies to be performed on sentiment and perception of information for the first time. In addition to the expectational data, recent work has been done in the laboratories led by the ground breaking work of Nobel Prize winner Vernon Smith. Going forward, more expectational data is being collected. The ability to use this data to judge sentiment in the marketplace will be crucial in improving our understanding of finance.

This book has focused on expectational earnings data. In 10 years, it is our hope that a new book can be written that will include studies and uses of expectational data on many other income statement items. Items like projected sales, projected cash flows, client sentiment, and others will allow us to look even more deeply into how human perceptions affect stock prices.

The field has come a long way since Brian Bruce co-edited *The Handbook of Corporate Earnings Analysis* in 1994, which was the first book put together on this topic. We hope this second book gives you an understanding of where we are today and ideas for proceeding into the future.